My name is

....

This is me

My first signature

....

All About Me

Name:

Address:

Parents Names / Contact Details:

	Tel:
	Tel:
Emergency Contact No.1	Tel:
Emergency Contact No.2	Tel:

Allergies:

Doctors: Tel:

Address:

Can I use Suncream?   Yes / No

☺ My Likes:

☹ My Dislikes:

😃 My Favourite Food & Snacks:

Additional Information

LINKS TO EYFS	What I Enjoyed Doing Today - Date:
☐ Self-Regulation	Planned Activities:
☐ Managing Self	
☐ Building Relationships	
☐ Listening, Attention and Understanding	
☐ Speaking	
☐ Gross Motor Skills	
☐ Fine Motor Skills	Spontaneous Activities:
☐ Comprehension	
☐ Word Reading	
☐ Writing	
☐ Number	
☐ Numerical Patterns	
☐ Past and Present	
☐ People, Culture and Communities	
☐ The Natural World	Key Achievement:
☐ Creating with Materials	
☐ Being Imaginative and Expressive	

Nappy Change or Toilet Visits	Time:		Time:		Time:		Time:	
	Wet ☐	Soiled ☐	Wet ☐	Soiled ☐	Wet ☐	Soiled ☐	Wet ☐	Soiled ☐

BOTTLES	Time	Duration	**SLEEPS**	From	To

Breakfast   Lunch   Teatime   Snacks

Parent / Carer Communication:

LINKS TO EYFS

- [ ] Self-Regulation
- [ ] Managing Self
- [ ] Building Relationships
- [ ] Listening, Attention and Understanding
- [ ] Speaking
- [ ] Gross Motor Skills
- [ ] Fine Motor Skills
- [ ] Comprehension
- [ ] Word Reading
- [ ] Writing
- [ ] Number
- [ ] Numerical Patterns
- [ ] Past and Present
- [ ] People, Culture and Communities
- [ ] The Natural World
- [ ] Creating with Materials
- [ ] Being Imaginative and Expressive

What I Enjoyed Doing Today - Date:

Planned Activities:

Spontaneous Activities:

Key Achievement:

Nappy Change or Toilet Visits	Time:		Time:		Time:		Time:	
	Wet	Soiled	Wet	Soiled	Wet	Soiled	Wet	Soiled
	[ ]	[ ]	[ ]	[ ]	[ ]	[ ]	[ ]	[ ]

BOTTLES   Time   Duration   **SLEEPS**   From   To

ᵇ Breakfast   ᵇ Lunch   ᵇ Teatime   ᵇ Snacks

Parent / Carer Communication:

LINKS TO EYFS

- [ ] Self-Regulation
- [ ] Managing Self
- [ ] Building Relationships
- [ ] Listening, Attention and Understanding
- [ ] Speaking
- [ ] Gross Motor Skills
- [ ] Fine Motor Skills
- [ ] Comprehension
- [ ] Word Reading
- [ ] Writing
- [ ] Number
- [ ] Numerical Patterns
- [ ] Past and Present
- [ ] People, Culture and Communities
- [ ] The Natural World
- [ ] Creating with Materials
- [ ] Being Imaginative and Expressive

What I Enjoyed Doing Today - Date:

Planned Activities:

Spontaneous Activities:

Key Achievement:

Nappy Change or Toilet Visits	Time:		Time:		Time:		Time:	
	Wet	Soiled	Wet	Soiled	Wet	Soiled	Wet	Soiled
	[ ]	[ ]	[ ]	[ ]	[ ]	[ ]	[ ]	[ ]

BOTTLES	Time	Duration	SLEEPS	From	To

Breakfast   Lunch   Teatime   Snacks

Parent / Carer Communication:

LINKS TO EYFS

- [ ] Self-Regulation
- [ ] Managing Self
- [ ] Building Relationships
- [ ] Listening, Attention and Understanding
- [ ] Speaking
- [ ] Gross Motor Skills
- [ ] Fine Motor Skills
- [ ] Comprehension
- [ ] Word Reading
- [ ] Writing
- [ ] Number
- [ ] Numerical Patterns
- [ ] Past and Present
- [ ] People, Culture and Communities
- [ ] The Natural World
- [ ] Creating with Materials
- [ ] Being Imaginative and Expressive

What I Enjoyed Doing Today - Date:

Planned Activities:

Spontaneous Activities:

Key Achievement:

Nappy Change / Toilet Visits

Time:		Time:		Time:		Time:	
Wet	Soiled	Wet	Soiled	Wet	Soiled	Wet	Soiled
☐	☐	☐	☐	☐	☐	☐	☐

BOTTLES	Time	Duration	SLEEPS	From	To

Breakfast   Lunch   Teatime   Snacks

Parent / Carer Communication:

LINKS TO EYFS	What I Enjoyed Doing Today - Date:
☐ Self-Regulation	**Planned Activities:**
☐ Managing Self	
☐ Building Relationships	
☐ Listening, Attention and Understanding	
☐ Speaking	
☐ Gross Motor Skills	
☐ Fine Motor Skills	**Spontaneous Activities:**
☐ Comprehension	
☐ Word Reading	
☐ Writing	
☐ Number	
☐ Numerical Patterns	
☐ Past and Present	
☐ People, Culture and Communities	
☐ The Natural World	**Key Achievement:**
☐ Creating with Materials	
☐ Being Imaginative and Expressive	

Nappy Change or Toilet Visits	Time:		Time:		Time:		Time:	
	Wet	Soiled	Wet	Soiled	Wet	Soiled	Wet	Soil
	☐	☐	☐	☐	☐	☐	☐	☐

BOTTLES	Time	Duration	**SLEEPS**	From	To

○ Breakfast   ○ Lunch   ○ Teatime   ○ Snacks

Parent / Carer Communication:

LINKS TO EYFS	What I Enjoyed Doing Today - Date:
☐ Self-Regulation ☐ Managing Self ☐ Building Relationships ☐ Listening, Attention and Understanding ☐ Speaking ☐ Gross Motor Skills ☐ Fine Motor Skills ☐ Comprehension ☐ Word Reading ☐ Writing ☐ Number ☐ Numerical Patterns ☐ Past and Present ☐ People, Culture and Communities ☐ The Natural World ☐ Creating with Materials ☐ Being Imaginative and Expressive	Planned Activities: Spontaneous Activities: Key Achievement:

Nappy Change or Toilet Visits	Time: Wet ☐	Soiled ☐	Time: Wet ☐	Soiled ☐	Time: Wet ☐	Soiled ☐	Time: Wet ☐	Soiled ☐

BOTTLES	Time	Duration	SLEEPS	From	To

○ Breakfast　　○ Lunch　　○ Teatime　　○ Snacks

Parent / Carer Communication:

LINKS TO EYFS

- ☐ Self-Regulation
- ☐ Managing Self
- ☐ Building Relationships
- ☐ Listening, Attention and Understanding
- ☐ Speaking
- ☐ Gross Motor Skills
- ☐ Fine Motor Skills
- ☐ Comprehension
- ☐ Word Reading
- ☐ Writing
- ☐ Number
- ☐ Numerical Patterns
- ☐ Past and Present
- ☐ People, Culture and Communities
- ☐ The Natural World
- ☐ Creating with Materials
- ☐ Being Imaginative and Expressive

What I Enjoyed Doing Today - Date:

Planned Activities:

Spontaneous Activities:

Key Achievement:

Nappy Change or Toilet Visits	Time:		Time:		Time:		Time:	
	Wet	Soiled	Wet	Soiled	Wet	Soiled	Wet	Soiled
	☐	☐	☐	☐	☐	☐	☐	☐

BOTTLES	Time	Duration	SLEEPS	From	To

Breakfast   Lunch   Teatime   Snacks

Parent / Carer Communication:

LINKS TO EYFS

- [ ] Self-Regulation
- [ ] Managing Self
- [ ] Building Relationships
- [ ] Listening, Attention and Understanding
- [ ] Speaking
- [ ] Gross Motor Skills
- [ ] Fine Motor Skills
- [ ] Comprehension
- [ ] Word Reading
- [ ] Writing
- [ ] Number
- [ ] Numerical Patterns
- [ ] Past and Present
- [ ] People, Culture and Communities
- [ ] The Natural World
- [ ] Creating with Materials
- [ ] Being Imaginative and Expressive

What I Enjoyed Doing Today - Date:

Planned Activities:

Spontaneous Activities:

Key Achievement:

Nappy Change or Toilet Visits	Time:		Time:		Time:		Time:	
	Wet	Soiled	Wet	Soiled	Wet	Soiled	Wet	Soiled
	[ ]	[ ]	[ ]	[ ]	[ ]	[ ]	[ ]	[ ]

BOTTLES	Time	Duration	**SLEEPS**	From	To

Breakfast   Lunch   Teatime   Snacks

Parent / Carer Communication:

LINKS TO EYFS

- [ ] Self-Regulation
- [ ] Managing Self
- [ ] Building Relationships
- [ ] Listening, Attention and Understanding
- [ ] Speaking
- [ ] Gross Motor Skills
- [ ] Fine Motor Skills
- [ ] Comprehension
- [ ] Word Reading
- [ ] Writing
- [ ] Number
- [ ] Numerical Patterns
- [ ] Past and Present
- [ ] People, Culture and Communities
- [ ] The Natural World
- [ ] Creating with Materials
- [ ] Being Imaginative and Expressive

What I Enjoyed Doing Today - Date:

Planned Activities:

Spontaneous Activities:

Key Achievement:

Nappy Change or Toilet Visits	Time:		Time:		Time:		Time:	
	Wet	Soiled	Wet	Soiled	Wet	Soiled	Wet	Soiled
	[ ]	[ ]	[ ]	[ ]	[ ]	[ ]	[ ]	[ ]

BOTTLES	Time	Duration	SLEEPS	From	To

Breakfast   Lunch   Teatime   Snacks

Parent / Carer Communication:

NKS TO EYFS	What I Enjoyed Doing Today - Date:

] Self-Regulation
] Managing Self
] Building Relationships
] Listening, Attention
   and Understanding
] Speaking
] Gross Motor Skills
] Fine Motor Skills
] Comprehension
] Word Reading
] Writing
] Number
] Numerical Patterns
] Past and Present
] People, Culture and
   Communities
] The Natural World
] Creating with Materials
] Being Imaginative and
   Expressive
	Planned Activities:
	
	Spontaneous Activities:
	
	Key Achievement:

appy Change	Time:		Time:		Time:		Time:	
Toilet Visits	Wet	Soiled	Wet	Soiled	Wet	Soiled	Wet	Soiled
	☐	☐	☐	☐	☐	☐	☐	☐

OTTLES	Time	Duration	**SLEEPS**	From	To

○ Breakfast	○ Lunch	○ Teatime	○ Snacks

rent / Carer Communication:

LINKS TO EYFS	What I Enjoyed Doing Today - Date:
☐ Self-Regulation ☐ Managing Self ☐ Building Relationships ☐ Listening, Attention and Understanding ☐ Speaking ☐ Gross Motor Skills ☐ Fine Motor Skills ☐ Comprehension ☐ Word Reading ☐ Writing ☐ Number ☐ Numerical Patterns ☐ Past and Present ☐ People, Culture and Communities ☐ The Natural World ☐ Creating with Materials ☐ Being Imaginative and Expressive	Planned Activities: Spontaneous Activities: Key Achievement:

Nappy Change or Toilet Visits	Time: Wet ☐	Soiled ☐	Time: Wet ☐	Soiled ☐	Time: Wet ☐	Soiled ☐	Time: Wet ☐	Soil ☐

BOTTLES	Time	Duration	**SLEEPS**	From	To

○ Breakfast	○ Lunch	○ Teatime	○ Snacks

Parent / Carer Communication:

LINKS TO EYFS	What I Enjoyed Doing Today - Date:

☐ Self-Regulation
☐ Managing Self
☐ Building Relationships
☐ Listening, Attention
   and Understanding
☐ Speaking
☐ Gross Motor Skills
☐ Fine Motor Skills
☐ Comprehension
☐ Word Reading
☐ Writing
☐ Number
☐ Numerical Patterns
☐ Past and Present
☐ People, Culture and
   Communities
☐ The Natural World
☐ Creating with Materials
☐ Being Imaginative and
   Expressive
	Planned Activities:
	
	Spontaneous Activities:
	
	Key Achievement:

Nappy Change or Toilet Visits	Time: Wet ☐	Soiled ☐	Time: Wet ☐	Soiled ☐	Time: Wet ☐	Soiled ☐	Time: Wet ☐	Soiled ☐

BOTTLES	Time	Duration	SLEEPS	From	To

Breakfast   Lunch   Teatime   Snacks

Parent / Carer Communication:

LINKS TO EYFS

- [ ] Self-Regulation
- [ ] Managing Self
- [ ] Building Relationships
- [ ] Listening, Attention and Understanding
- [ ] Speaking
- [ ] Gross Motor Skills
- [ ] Fine Motor Skills
- [ ] Comprehension
- [ ] Word Reading
- [ ] Writing
- [ ] Number
- [ ] Numerical Patterns
- [ ] Past and Present
- [ ] People, Culture and Communities
- [ ] The Natural World
- [ ] Creating with Materials
- [ ] Being Imaginative and Expressive

What I Enjoyed Doing Today - Date:

Planned Activities:

Spontaneous Activities:

Key Achievement:

Nappy Change or Toilet Visits

	Time:		Time:		Time:		Time:	
	Wet	Soiled	Wet	Soiled	Wet	Soiled	Wet	Soiled
	☐	☐	☐	☐	☐	☐	☐	☐

BOTTLES	Time	Duration	SLEEPS	From	To

○ Breakfast   ○ Lunch   ○ Teatime   ○ Snacks

Parent / Carer Communication:

LINKS TO EYFS	What I Enjoyed Doing Today - Date:
☐ Self-Regulation ☐ Managing Self ☐ Building Relationships ☐ Listening, Attention and Understanding ☐ Speaking ☐ Gross Motor Skills ☐ Fine Motor Skills ☐ Comprehension ☐ Word Reading ☐ Writing ☐ Number ☐ Numerical Patterns ☐ Past and Present ☐ People, Culture and Communities ☐ The Natural World ☐ Creating with Materials ☐ Being Imaginative and Expressive	Planned Activities: Spontaneous Activities: Key Achievement:

Nappy Change or Toilet Visits	Time: Wet ☐ Soiled ☐	Time: Wet ☐ Soiled ☐	Time: Wet ☐ Soiled ☐	Time: Wet ☐ Soiled ☐

BOTTLES	Time	Duration	**SLEEPS**	From	To

○ Breakfast   ○ Lunch   ○ Teatime   ○ Snacks

Parent / Carer Communication:

LINKS TO EYFS

- [ ] Self-Regulation
- [ ] Managing Self
- [ ] Building Relationships
- [ ] Listening, Attention and Understanding
- [ ] Speaking
- [ ] Gross Motor Skills
- [ ] Fine Motor Skills
- [ ] Comprehension
- [ ] Word Reading
- [ ] Writing
- [ ] Number
- [ ] Numerical Patterns
- [ ] Past and Present
- [ ] People, Culture and Communities
- [ ] The Natural World
- [ ] Creating with Materials
- [ ] Being Imaginative and Expressive

What I Enjoyed Doing Today - Date:

Planned Activities:

Spontaneous Activities:

Key Achievement:

Nappy Change or Toilet Visits	Time:		Time:		Time:		Time:	
	Wet	Soiled	Wet	Soiled	Wet	Soiled	Wet	Soiled
	[ ]	[ ]	[ ]	[ ]	[ ]	[ ]	[ ]	[ ]

BOTTLES	Time	Duration	**SLEEPS**	From	To

- Breakfast
- Lunch
- Teatime
- Snacks

Parent / Carer Communication:

NKS TO EYFS

] Self-Regulation
] Managing Self
] Building Relationships
] Listening, Attention
  and Understanding
] Speaking
] Gross Motor Skills
] Fine Motor Skills
] Comprehension
] Word Reading
] Writing
] Number
] Numerical Patterns
] Past and Present
] People, Culture and
  Communities
] The Natural World
] Creating with Materials
] Being Imaginative and
  Expressive

What I Enjoyed Doing Today - Date:

Planned Activities:

Spontaneous Activities:

Key Achievement:

appy Change Toilet Visits	Time:		Time:		Time:		Time:	
	Wet	Soiled	Wet	Soiled	Wet	Soiled	Wet	Soiled
	☐	☐	☐	☐	☐	☐	☐	☐

OTTLES	Time	Duration	SLEEPS	From	To

Breakfast   Lunch   Teatime   Snacks

rent / Carer Communication:

LINKS TO EYFS	What I Enjoyed Doing Today - Date:

LINKS TO EYFS

- [ ] Self-Regulation
- [ ] Managing Self
- [ ] Building Relationships
- [ ] Listening, Attention and Understanding
- [ ] Speaking
- [ ] Gross Motor Skills
- [ ] Fine Motor Skills
- [ ] Comprehension
- [ ] Word Reading
- [ ] Writing
- [ ] Number
- [ ] Numerical Patterns
- [ ] Past and Present
- [ ] People, Culture and Communities
- [ ] The Natural World
- [ ] Creating with Materials
- [ ] Being Imaginative and Expressive

Planned Activities:

Spontaneous Activities:

Key Achievement:

Nappy Change or Toilet Visits	Time:		Time:		Time:		Time:	
	Wet	Soiled	Wet	Soiled	Wet	Soiled	Wet	Soil
	[ ]	[ ]	[ ]	[ ]	[ ]	[ ]	[ ]	[ ]

BOTTLES	Time	Duration	SLEEPS	From	To

○ Breakfast   ○ Lunch   ○ Teatime   ○ Snacks

Parent / Carer Communication:

LINKS TO EYFS	What I Enjoyed Doing Today - Date:
☐ Self-Regulation ☐ Managing Self ☐ Building Relationships ☐ Listening, Attention and Understanding ☐ Speaking ☐ Gross Motor Skills ☐ Fine Motor Skills ☐ Comprehension ☐ Word Reading ☐ Writing ☐ Number ☐ Numerical Patterns ☐ Past and Present ☐ People, Culture and Communities ☐ The Natural World ☐ Creating with Materials ☐ Being Imaginative and Expressive	Planned Activities: Spontaneous Activities: Key Achievement:

Nappy Change or Toilet Visits	Time:		Time:		Time:		Time:	
	Wet	Soiled	Wet	Soiled	Wet	Soiled	Wet	Soiled
	☐	☐	☐	☐	☐	☐	☐	☐

BOTTLES	Time	Duration	SLEEPS	From	To

Breakfast	Lunch	Teatime	Snacks

Parent / Carer Communication:

LINKS TO EYFS

- [ ] Self-Regulation
- [ ] Managing Self
- [ ] Building Relationships
- [ ] Listening, Attention and Understanding
- [ ] Speaking
- [ ] Gross Motor Skills
- [ ] Fine Motor Skills
- [ ] Comprehension
- [ ] Word Reading
- [ ] Writing
- [ ] Number
- [ ] Numerical Patterns
- [ ] Past and Present
- [ ] People, Culture and Communities
- [ ] The Natural World
- [ ] Creating with Materials
- [ ] Being Imaginative and Expressive

What I Enjoyed Doing Today - Date:

Planned Activities:

Spontaneous Activities:

Key Achievement:

Nappy Change or Toilet Visits	Time:		Time:		Time:		Time:	
	Wet	Soiled	Wet	Soiled	Wet	Soiled	Wet	Soiled
	[ ]	[ ]	[ ]	[ ]	[ ]	[ ]	[ ]	[ ]

BOTTLES	Time	Duration	SLEEPS	From	To

Breakfast	Lunch	Teatime	Snacks

Parent / Carer Communication:

LINKS TO EYFS	What I Enjoyed Doing Today - Date:

☐ Self-Regulation
☐ Managing Self
☐ Building Relationships
☐ Listening, Attention
   and Understanding
☐ Speaking
☐ Gross Motor Skills
☐ Fine Motor Skills
☐ Comprehension
☐ Word Reading
☐ Writing
☐ Number
☐ Numerical Patterns
☐ Past and Present
☐ People, Culture and
   Communities
☐ The Natural World
☐ Creating with Materials
☐ Being Imaginative and
   Expressive

Planned Activities:

Spontaneous Activities:

Key Achievement:

Nappy Change or Toilet Visits	Time:		Time:		Time:		Time:	
	Wet	Soiled	Wet	Soiled	Wet	Soiled	Wet	Soiled
	☐	☐	☐	☐	☐	☐	☐	☐

BOTTLES	Time	Duration	**SLEEPS**	From	To

Breakfast	Lunch	Teatime	Snacks

Parent / Carer Communication:

LINKS TO EYFS

- ☐ Self-Regulation
- ☐ Managing Self
- ☐ Building Relationships
- ☐ Listening, Attention and Understanding
- ☐ Speaking
- ☐ Gross Motor Skills
- ☐ Fine Motor Skills
- ☐ Comprehension
- ☐ Word Reading
- ☐ Writing
- ☐ Number
- ☐ Numerical Patterns
- ☐ Past and Present
- ☐ People, Culture and Communities
- ☐ The Natural World
- ☐ Creating with Materials
- ☐ Being Imaginative and Expressive

What I Enjoyed Doing Today - Date:

Planned Activities:

Spontaneous Activities:

Key Achievement:

Nappy Change or Toilet Visits	Time:		Time:		Time:		Time:	
	Wet	Soiled	Wet	Soiled	Wet	Soiled	Wet	Soiled
	☐	☐	☐	☐	☐	☐	☐	☐

BOTTLES	Time	Duration	SLEEPS	From	To

Breakfast	Lunch	Teatime	Snacks

Parent / Carer Communication:

NKS TO EYFS | What I Enjoyed Doing Today - Date:

] Self-Regulation
] Managing Self
] Building Relationships
] Listening, Attention
  and Understanding
] Speaking
] Gross Motor Skills
] Fine Motor Skills
] Comprehension
] Word Reading
] Writing
] Number
] Numerical Patterns
] Past and Present
] People, Culture and
  Communities
] The Natural World
] Creating with Materials
] Being Imaginative and
  Expressive

Planned Activities:

Spontaneous Activities:

Key Achievement:

appy Change	Time:		Time:		Time:		Time:	
	Wet	Soiled	Wet	Soiled	Wet	Soiled	Wet	Soiled
Toilet Visits	☐	☐	☐	☐	☐	☐	☐	☐

OTTLES	Time	Duration	**SLEEPS**	From	To

Breakfast   Lunch   Teatime   Snacks

rent / Carer Communication:

LINKS TO EYFS	What I Enjoyed Doing Today - Date:
☐ Self-Regulation	Planned Activities:
☐ Managing Self	
☐ Building Relationships	
☐ Listening, Attention and Understanding	
☐ Speaking	
☐ Gross Motor Skills	
☐ Fine Motor Skills	Spontaneous Activities:
☐ Comprehension	
☐ Word Reading	
☐ Writing	
☐ Number	
☐ Numerical Patterns	
☐ Past and Present	
☐ People, Culture and Communities	
☐ The Natural World	Key Achievement:
☐ Creating with Materials	
☐ Being Imaginative and Expressive	

Nappy Change or Toilet Visits	Time:		Time:		Time:		Time:	
	Wet	Soiled	Wet	Soiled	Wet	Soiled	Wet	Soil
	☐	☐	☐	☐	☐	☐	☐	☐

BOTTLES	Time	Duration	SLEEPS	From	To

o Breakfast   o Lunch   o Teatime   o Snacks

Parent / Carer Communication:

LINKS TO EYFS	What I Enjoyed Doing Today - Date:
☐ Self-Regulation ☐ Managing Self ☐ Building Relationships ☐ Listening, Attention and Understanding ☐ Speaking ☐ Gross Motor Skills ☐ Fine Motor Skills ☐ Comprehension ☐ Word Reading ☐ Writing ☐ Number ☐ Numerical Patterns ☐ Past and Present ☐ People, Culture and Communities ☐ The Natural World ☐ Creating with Materials ☐ Being Imaginative and Expressive	Planned Activities: Spontaneous Activities: Key Achievement:

Nappy Change or Toilet Visits	Time:		Time:		Time:		Time:	
	Wet ☐	Soiled ☐	Wet ☐	Soiled ☐	Wet ☐	Soiled ☐	Wet ☐	Soiled ☐

BOTTLES	Time	Duration	**SLEEPS**	From	To

○ Breakfast	○ Lunch	○ Teatime	○ Snacks

Parent / Carer Communication:

LINKS TO EYFS

What I Enjoyed Doing Today - Date:

- [ ] Self-Regulation
- [ ] Managing Self
- [ ] Building Relationships
- [ ] Listening, Attention and Understanding
- [ ] Speaking
- [ ] Gross Motor Skills
- [ ] Fine Motor Skills
- [ ] Comprehension
- [ ] Word Reading
- [ ] Writing
- [ ] Number
- [ ] Numerical Patterns
- [ ] Past and Present
- [ ] People, Culture and Communities
- [ ] The Natural World
- [ ] Creating with Materials
- [ ] Being Imaginative and Expressive

Planned Activities:

Spontaneous Activities:

Key Achievement:

Nappy Change or Toilet Visits	Time:		Time:		Time:		Time:	
	Wet	Soiled	Wet	Soiled	Wet	Soiled	Wet	Soiled
	[ ]	[ ]	[ ]	[ ]	[ ]	[ ]	[ ]	[ ]

BOTTLES	Time	Duration	SLEEPS	From	To

Breakfast　　Lunch　　Teatime　　Snacks

Parent / Carer Communication:

LINKS TO EYFS	What I Enjoyed Doing Today - Date:

LINKS TO EYFS

☐ Self-Regulation
☐ Managing Self
☐ Building Relationships
☐ Listening, Attention
   and Understanding
☐ Speaking
☐ Gross Motor Skills
☐ Fine Motor Skills
☐ Comprehension
☐ Word Reading
☐ Writing
☐ Number
☐ Numerical Patterns
☐ Past and Present
☐ People, Culture and
   Communities
☐ The Natural World
☐ Creating with Materials
☐ Being Imaginative and
   Expressive

Planned Activities:

Spontaneous Activities:

Key Achievement:

Nappy Change or Toilet Visits	Time:		Time:		Time:		Time:	
	Wet	Soiled	Wet	Soiled	Wet	Soiled	Wet	Soiled
	☐	☐	☐	☐	☐	☐	☐	☐

BOTTLES   Time   Duration   **SLEEPS**   From   To

ỏ Breakfast   ỏ Lunch   ỏ Teatime   ỏ Snacks

Parent / Carer Communication:

LINKS TO EYFS

- [ ] Self-Regulation
- [ ] Managing Self
- [ ] Building Relationships
- [ ] Listening, Attention and Understanding
- [ ] Speaking
- [ ] Gross Motor Skills
- [ ] Fine Motor Skills
- [ ] Comprehension
- [ ] Word Reading
- [ ] Writing
- [ ] Number
- [ ] Numerical Patterns
- [ ] Past and Present
- [ ] People, Culture and Communities
- [ ] The Natural World
- [ ] Creating with Materials
- [ ] Being Imaginative and Expressive

What I Enjoyed Doing Today - Date:

Planned Activities:

Spontaneous Activities:

Key Achievement:

Nappy Change or Toilet Visits	Time:		Time:		Time:		Time:	
	Wet	Soiled	Wet	Soiled	Wet	Soiled	Wet	Soiled
	[ ]	[ ]	[ ]	[ ]	[ ]	[ ]	[ ]	[ ]

BOTTLES	Time	Duration	SLEEPS	From	To

Breakfast   Lunch   Teatime   Snacks

Parent / Carer Communication:

NKS TO EYFS

- [ ] Self-Regulation
- [ ] Managing Self
- [ ] Building Relationships
- [ ] Listening, Attention and Understanding
- [ ] Speaking
- [ ] Gross Motor Skills
- [ ] Fine Motor Skills
- [ ] Comprehension
- [ ] Word Reading
- [ ] Writing
- [ ] Number
- [ ] Numerical Patterns
- [ ] Past and Present
- [ ] People, Culture and Communities
- [ ] The Natural World
- [ ] Creating with Materials
- [ ] Being Imaginative and Expressive

What I Enjoyed Doing Today - Date:

Planned Activities:

Spontaneous Activities:

Key Achievement:

Nappy Change Toilet Visits	Time:		Time:		Time:		Time:	
	Wet	Soiled	Wet	Soiled	Wet	Soiled	Wet	Soiled
	☐	☐	☐	☐	☐	☐	☐	☐

BOTTLES	Time	Duration	SLEEPS	From	To

Breakfast   Lunch   Teatime   Snacks

Parent / Carer Communication:

LINKS TO EYFS

- [ ] Self-Regulation
- [ ] Managing Self
- [ ] Building Relationships
- [ ] Listening, Attention and Understanding
- [ ] Speaking
- [ ] Gross Motor Skills
- [ ] Fine Motor Skills
- [ ] Comprehension
- [ ] Word Reading
- [ ] Writing
- [ ] Number
- [ ] Numerical Patterns
- [ ] Past and Present
- [ ] People, Culture and Communities
- [ ] The Natural World
- [ ] Creating with Materials
- [ ] Being Imaginative and Expressive

What I Enjoyed Doing Today - Date:

Planned Activities:

Spontaneous Activities:

Key Achievement:

Nappy Change or Toilet Visits	Time:		Time:		Time:		Time:	
	Wet	Soiled	Wet	Soiled	Wet	Soiled	Wet	Soil
	[ ]	[ ]	[ ]	[ ]	[ ]	[ ]	[ ]	[ ]

BOTTLES	Time	Duration	**SLEEPS**	From	To

Breakfast   Lunch   Teatime   Snacks

Parent / Carer Communication:

LINKS TO EYFS	What I Enjoyed Doing Today - Date:
☐ Self-Regulation ☐ Managing Self ☐ Building Relationships ☐ Listening, Attention and Understanding ☐ Speaking ☐ Gross Motor Skills ☐ Fine Motor Skills ☐ Comprehension ☐ Word Reading ☐ Writing ☐ Number ☐ Numerical Patterns ☐ Past and Present ☐ People, Culture and Communities ☐ The Natural World ☐ Creating with Materials ☐ Being Imaginative and Expressive	Planned Activities: Spontaneous Activities: Key Achievement:

Nappy Change or Toilet Visits	Time:		Time:		Time:		Time:	
	Wet	Soiled	Wet	Soiled	Wet	Soiled	Wet	Soiled
	☐	☐	☐	☐	☐	☐	☐	☐

BOTTLES	Time	Duration	SLEEPS	From	To

Breakfast   Lunch   Teatime   Snacks

Parent / Carer Communication:

LINKS TO EYFS

- [ ] Self-Regulation
- [ ] Managing Self
- [ ] Building Relationships
- [ ] Listening, Attention and Understanding
- [ ] Speaking
- [ ] Gross Motor Skills
- [ ] Fine Motor Skills
- [ ] Comprehension
- [ ] Word Reading
- [ ] Writing
- [ ] Number
- [ ] Numerical Patterns
- [ ] Past and Present
- [ ] People, Culture and Communities
- [ ] The Natural World
- [ ] Creating with Materials
- [ ] Being Imaginative and Expressive

What I Enjoyed Doing Today - Date:

Planned Activities:

Spontaneous Activities:

Key Achievement:

Nappy Change or Toilet Visits	Time:		Time:		Time:		Time:	
	Wet	Soiled	Wet	Soiled	Wet	Soiled	Wet	Soiled
	[ ]	[ ]	[ ]	[ ]	[ ]	[ ]	[ ]	[ ]

BOTTLES	Time	Duration	SLEEPS	From	To

○ Breakfast	○ Lunch	○ Teatime	○ Snacks

Parent / Carer Communication:

LINKS TO EYFS	What I Enjoyed Doing Today - Date:

LINKS TO EYFS

☐ Self-Regulation
☐ Managing Self
☐ Building Relationships
☐ Listening, Attention
   and Understanding
☐ Speaking
☐ Gross Motor Skills
☐ Fine Motor Skills
☐ Comprehension
☐ Word Reading
☐ Writing
☐ Number
☐ Numerical Patterns
☐ Past and Present
☐ People, Culture and
   Communities
☐ The Natural World
☐ Creating with Materials
☐ Being Imaginative and
   Expressive

Planned Activities:

Spontaneous Activities:

Key Achievement:

Nappy Change or Toilet Visits	Time:		Time:		Time:		Time:	
	Wet	Soiled	Wet	Soiled	Wet	Soiled	Wet	Soiled
	☐	☐	☐	☐	☐	☐	☐	☐

BOTTLES	Time	Duration	**SLEEPS**	From	To

Breakfast   Lunch   Teatime   Snacks

Parent / Carer Communication:

LINKS TO EYFS

- ☐ Self-Regulation
- ☐ Managing Self
- ☐ Building Relationships
- ☐ Listening, Attention and Understanding
- ☐ Speaking
- ☐ Gross Motor Skills
- ☐ Fine Motor Skills
- ☐ Comprehension
- ☐ Word Reading
- ☐ Writing
- ☐ Number
- ☐ Numerical Patterns
- ☐ Past and Present
- ☐ People, Culture and Communities
- ☐ The Natural World
- ☐ Creating with Materials
- ☐ Being Imaginative and Expressive

What I Enjoyed Doing Today - Date:

Planned Activities:

Spontaneous Activities:

Key Achievement:

Nappy Change or Toilet Visits	Time:		Time:		Time:		Time:	
	Wet	Soiled	Wet	Soiled	Wet	Soiled	Wet	Soiled
	☐	☐	☐	☐	☐	☐	☐	☐

BOTTLES	Time	Duration	SLEEPS	From	To

○ Breakfast   ○ Lunch   ○ Teatime   ○ Snacks

Parent / Carer Communication:

NKS TO EYFS

] Self-Regulation
] Managing Self
] Building Relationships
] Listening, Attention
  and Understanding
] Speaking
] Gross Motor Skills
] Fine Motor Skills
] Comprehension
] Word Reading
] Writing
] Number
] Numerical Patterns
] Past and Present
] People, Culture and
  Communities
] The Natural World
] Creating with Materials
] Being Imaginative and
  Expressive

What I Enjoyed Doing Today - Date:

Planned Activities:

Spontaneous Activities:

Key Achievement:

appy Change Toilet Visits	Time:		Time:		Time:		Time:	
	Wet	Soiled	Wet	Soiled	Wet	Soiled	Wet	Soiled
	☐	☐	☐	☐	☐	☐	☐	☐

OTTLES	Time	Duration	**SLEEPS**	From	To

Breakfast   Lunch   Teatime   Snacks

rent / Carer Communication:

LINKS TO EYFS

- [ ] Self-Regulation
- [ ] Managing Self
- [ ] Building Relationships
- [ ] Listening, Attention and Understanding
- [ ] Speaking
- [ ] Gross Motor Skills
- [ ] Fine Motor Skills
- [ ] Comprehension
- [ ] Word Reading
- [ ] Writing
- [ ] Number
- [ ] Numerical Patterns
- [ ] Past and Present
- [ ] People, Culture and Communities
- [ ] The Natural World
- [ ] Creating with Materials
- [ ] Being Imaginative and Expressive

What I Enjoyed Doing Today - Date:

Planned Activities:

Spontaneous Activities:

Key Achievement:

Nappy Change or Toilet Visits	Time:		Time:		Time:		Time:	
	Wet	Soiled	Wet	Soiled	Wet	Soiled	Wet	Soil
	[ ]	[ ]	[ ]	[ ]	[ ]	[ ]	[ ]	[ ]

BOTTLES	Time	Duration	SLEEPS	From	To

○ Breakfast   ○ Lunch   ○ Teatime   ○ Snacks

Parent / Carer Communication:

LINKS TO EYFS

- ☐ Self-Regulation
- ☐ Managing Self
- ☐ Building Relationships
- ☐ Listening, Attention and Understanding
- ☐ Speaking
- ☐ Gross Motor Skills
- ☐ Fine Motor Skills
- ☐ Comprehension
- ☐ Word Reading
- ☐ Writing
- ☐ Number
- ☐ Numerical Patterns
- ☐ Past and Present
- ☐ People, Culture and Communities
- ☐ The Natural World
- ☐ Creating with Materials
- ☐ Being Imaginative and Expressive

What I Enjoyed Doing Today - Date:

Planned Activities:

Spontaneous Activities:

Key Achievement:

Nappy Change or Toilet Visits	Time:		Time:		Time:		Time:	
	Wet	Soiled	Wet	Soiled	Wet	Soiled	Wet	Soiled
	☐	☐	☐	☐	☐	☐	☐	☐

BOTTLES	Time	Duration	SLEEPS	From	To

Breakfast   Lunch   Teatime   Snacks

Parent / Carer Communication:

LINKS TO EYFS

- [ ] Self-Regulation
- [ ] Managing Self
- [ ] Building Relationships
- [ ] Listening, Attention and Understanding
- [ ] Speaking
- [ ] Gross Motor Skills
- [ ] Fine Motor Skills
- [ ] Comprehension
- [ ] Word Reading
- [ ] Writing
- [ ] Number
- [ ] Numerical Patterns
- [ ] Past and Present
- [ ] People, Culture and Communities
- [ ] The Natural World
- [ ] Creating with Materials
- [ ] Being Imaginative and Expressive

What I Enjoyed Doing Today - Date:

Planned Activities:

Spontaneous Activities:

Key Achievement:

Nappy Change or Toilet Visits	Time:		Time:		Time:		Time:	
	Wet	Soiled	Wet	Soiled	Wet	Soiled	Wet	Soiled
	[ ]	[ ]	[ ]	[ ]	[ ]	[ ]	[ ]	[ ]

BOTTLES	Time	Duration	SLEEPS	From	To

Breakfast   Lunch   Teatime   Snacks

Parent / Carer Communication:

LINKS TO EYFS	What I Enjoyed Doing Today - Date:

☐ Self-Regulation
☐ Managing Self
☐ Building Relationships
☐ Listening, Attention
   and Understanding
☐ Speaking
☐ Gross Motor Skills
☐ Fine Motor Skills
☐ Comprehension
☐ Word Reading
☐ Writing
☐ Number
☐ Numerical Patterns
☐ Past and Present
☐ People, Culture and
   Communities
☐ The Natural World
☐ Creating with Materials
☐ Being Imaginative and
   Expressive
	Planned Activities:
	
	Spontaneous Activities:
	
	Key Achievement:

Nappy Change or Toilet Visits	Time: Wet ☐	Soiled ☐	Time: Wet ☐	Soiled ☐	Time: Wet ☐	Soiled ☐	Time: Wet ☐	Soiled ☐

BOTTLES	Time	Duration	SLEEPS	From	To

○ Breakfast	○ Lunch	○ Teatime	○ Snacks

Parent / Carer Communication:

LINKS TO EYFS

- [ ] Self-Regulation
- [ ] Managing Self
- [ ] Building Relationships
- [ ] Listening, Attention and Understanding
- [ ] Speaking
- [ ] Gross Motor Skills
- [ ] Fine Motor Skills
- [ ] Comprehension
- [ ] Word Reading
- [ ] Writing
- [ ] Number
- [ ] Numerical Patterns
- [ ] Past and Present
- [ ] People, Culture and Communities
- [ ] The Natural World
- [ ] Creating with Materials
- [ ] Being Imaginative and Expressive

What I Enjoyed Doing Today - Date:

Planned Activities:

Spontaneous Activities:

Key Achievement:

Nappy Change or Toilet Visits	Time:		Time:		Time:		Time:	
	Wet	Soiled	Wet	Soiled	Wet	Soiled	Wet	Soiled
	[ ]	[ ]	[ ]	[ ]	[ ]	[ ]	[ ]	[ ]

BOTTLES	Time	Duration	**SLEEPS**	From	To

Breakfast   Lunch   Teatime   Snacks

Parent / Carer Communication:

NKS TO EYFS	What I Enjoyed Doing Today - Date:
] Self-Regulation	**Planned Activities:**
] Managing Self	
] Building Relationships	
] Listening, Attention and Understanding	
] Speaking	
] Gross Motor Skills	
] Fine Motor Skills	**Spontaneous Activities:**
] Comprehension	
] Word Reading	
] Writing	
] Number	
] Numerical Patterns	
] Past and Present	
] People, Culture and Communities	
] The Natural World	**Key Achievement:**
] Creating with Materials	
] Being Imaginative and Expressive	

appy Change	Time:		Time:		Time:		Time:	
	Wet	Soiled	Wet	Soiled	Wet	Soiled	Wet	Soiled
Toilet Visits	☐	☐	☐	☐	☐	☐	☐	☐

OTTLES	Time	Duration	**SLEEPS**	From	To

Breakfast	Lunch	Teatime	Snacks

rent / Carer Communication:

LINKS TO EYFS	What I Enjoyed Doing Today - Date:
☐ Self-Regulation ☐ Managing Self ☐ Building Relationships ☐ Listening, Attention and Understanding ☐ Speaking ☐ Gross Motor Skills ☐ Fine Motor Skills ☐ Comprehension ☐ Word Reading ☐ Writing ☐ Number ☐ Numerical Patterns ☐ Past and Present ☐ People, Culture and Communities ☐ The Natural World ☐ Creating with Materials ☐ Being Imaginative and Expressive	Planned Activities: Spontaneous Activities: Key Achievement:

Nappy Change or Toilet Visits	Time: Wet ☐	Soiled ☐	Time: Wet ☐	Soiled ☐	Time: Wet ☐	Soiled ☐	Time: Wet ☐	Soil ☐

BOTTLES	Time	Duration	**SLEEPS**	From	To

○ Breakfast	○ Lunch	○ Teatime	○ Snacks

Parent / Carer Communication:

LINKS TO EYFS	What I Enjoyed Doing Today - Date:

☐ Self-Regulation
☐ Managing Self
☐ Building Relationships
☐ Listening, Attention
  and Understanding
☐ Speaking
☐ Gross Motor Skills
☐ Fine Motor Skills
☐ Comprehension
☐ Word Reading
☐ Writing
☐ Number
☐ Numerical Patterns
☐ Past and Present
☐ People, Culture and
  Communities
☐ The Natural World
☐ Creating with Materials
☐ Being Imaginative and
  Expressive
	Planned Activities:
	
	Spontaneous Activities:
	
	Key Achievement:

Nappy Change or Toilet Visits	Time: Wet ☐	Soiled ☐	Time: Wet ☐	Soiled ☐	Time: Wet ☐	Soiled ☐	Time: Wet ☐	Soiled ☐

BOTTLES	Time	Duration	SLEEPS	From	To

ᵒ Breakfast   ᵒ Lunch   ᵒ Teatime   ᵒ Snacks

Parent / Carer Communication:

LINKS TO EYFS	What I Enjoyed Doing Today - Date:

☐ Self-Regulation
☐ Managing Self
☐ Building Relationships
☐ Listening, Attention
  and Understanding
☐ Speaking
☐ Gross Motor Skills
☐ Fine Motor Skills
☐ Comprehension
☐ Word Reading
☐ Writing
☐ Number
☐ Numerical Patterns
☐ Past and Present
☐ People, Culture and
  Communities
☐ The Natural World
☐ Creating with Materials
☐ Being Imaginative and
  Expressive
	Planned Activities:
	
	Spontaneous Activities:
	
	Key Achievement:

Nappy Change or Toilet Visits	Time: Wet ☐ Soiled ☐	Time: Wet ☐ Soiled ☐	Time: Wet ☐ Soiled ☐	Time: Wet ☐ Soiled ☐

BOTTLES	Time	Duration	SLEEPS	From	To

○ Breakfast   ○ Lunch   ○ Teatime   ○ Snacks

Parent / Carer Communication:

LINKS TO EYFS

- ☐ Self-Regulation
- ☐ Managing Self
- ☐ Building Relationships
- ☐ Listening, Attention and Understanding
- ☐ Speaking
- ☐ Gross Motor Skills
- ☐ Fine Motor Skills
- ☐ Comprehension
- ☐ Word Reading
- ☐ Writing
- ☐ Number
- ☐ Numerical Patterns
- ☐ Past and Present
- ☐ People, Culture and Communities
- ☐ The Natural World
- ☐ Creating with Materials
- ☐ Being Imaginative and Expressive

What I Enjoyed Doing Today - Date:

Planned Activities:

Spontaneous Activities:

Key Achievement:

Nappy Change or Toilet Visits	Time:		Time:		Time:		Time:	
	Wet	Soiled	Wet	Soiled	Wet	Soiled	Wet	Soiled
	☐	☐	☐	☐	☐	☐	☐	☐

BOTTLES	Time	Duration	**SLEEPS**	From	To

○ Breakfast   ○ Lunch   ○ Teatime   ○ Snacks

Parent / Carer Communication:

LINKS TO EYFS

- [ ] Self-Regulation
- [ ] Managing Self
- [ ] Building Relationships
- [ ] Listening, Attention and Understanding
- [ ] Speaking
- [ ] Gross Motor Skills
- [ ] Fine Motor Skills
- [ ] Comprehension
- [ ] Word Reading
- [ ] Writing
- [ ] Number
- [ ] Numerical Patterns
- [ ] Past and Present
- [ ] People, Culture and Communities
- [ ] The Natural World
- [ ] Creating with Materials
- [ ] Being Imaginative and Expressive

What I Enjoyed Doing Today - Date:

Planned Activities:

Spontaneous Activities:

Key Achievement:

Nappy Change or Toilet Visits	Time:		Time:		Time:		Time:	
	Wet	Soiled	Wet	Soiled	Wet	Soiled	Wet	Soiled
	[ ]	[ ]	[ ]	[ ]	[ ]	[ ]	[ ]	[ ]

BOTTLES	Time	Duration	**SLEEPS**	From	To

ⵔ Breakfast   ⵔ Lunch   ⵔ Teatime   ⵔ Snacks

Parent / Carer Communication:

NKS TO EYFS | What I Enjoyed Doing Today - Date:

Self-Regulation
Managing Self
Building Relationships
Listening, Attention
and Understanding
Speaking
Gross Motor Skills
Fine Motor Skills
Comprehension
Word Reading
Writing
Number
Numerical Patterns
Past and Present
People, Culture and
Communities
The Natural World
Creating with Materials
Being Imaginative and
Expressive

Planned Activities:

Spontaneous Activities:

Key Achievement:

ippy Change Toilet Visits	Time: Wet	Soiled	Time: Wet	Soiled	Time: Wet	Soiled	Time: Wet	Soiled
	☐	☐	☐	☐	☐	☐	☐	☐

OTTLES	Time	Duration	**SLEEPS**	From	To

Breakfast   Lunch   Teatime   Snacks

rent / Carer Communication:

LINKS TO EYFS	What I Enjoyed Doing Today - Date:
☐ Self-Regulation	Planned Activities:
☐ Managing Self	
☐ Building Relationships	
☐ Listening, Attention and Understanding	
☐ Speaking	
☐ Gross Motor Skills	
☐ Fine Motor Skills	Spontaneous Activities:
☐ Comprehension	
☐ Word Reading	
☐ Writing	
☐ Number	
☐ Numerical Patterns	
☐ Past and Present	
☐ People, Culture and Communities	
☐ The Natural World	Key Achievement:
☐ Creating with Materials	
☐ Being Imaginative and Expressive	

Nappy Change or Toilet Visits	Time:		Time:		Time:		Time:	
	Wet	Soiled	Wet	Soiled	Wet	Soiled	Wet	Soil
	☐	☐	☐	☐	☐	☐	☐	☐

BOTTLES	Time	Duration	**SLEEPS**	From	To

Breakfast	Lunch	Teatime	Snacks

Parent / Carer Communication:

LINKS TO EYFS	What I Enjoyed Doing Today - Date:
☐ Self-Regulation ☐ Managing Self ☐ Building Relationships ☐ Listening, Attention and Understanding ☐ Speaking ☐ Gross Motor Skills ☐ Fine Motor Skills ☐ Comprehension ☐ Word Reading ☐ Writing ☐ Number ☐ Numerical Patterns ☐ Past and Present ☐ People, Culture and Communities ☐ The Natural World ☐ Creating with Materials ☐ Being Imaginative and Expressive	Planned Activities: Spontaneous Activities: Key Achievement:

Nappy Change or Toilet Visits	Time: Wet ☐	Soiled ☐	Time: Wet ☐	Soiled ☐	Time: Wet ☐	Soiled ☐	Time: Wet ☐	Soiled ☐

BOTTLES	Time	Duration	SLEEPS	From	To

○ Breakfast	○ Lunch	○ Teatime	○ Snacks

Parent / Carer Communication:

LINKS TO EYFS	What I Enjoyed Doing Today - Date:
☐ Self-Regulation ☐ Managing Self ☐ Building Relationships ☐ Listening, Attention and Understanding ☐ Speaking ☐ Gross Motor Skills ☐ Fine Motor Skills ☐ Comprehension ☐ Word Reading ☐ Writing ☐ Number ☐ Numerical Patterns ☐ Past and Present ☐ People, Culture and Communities ☐ The Natural World ☐ Creating with Materials ☐ Being Imaginative and Expressive	Planned Activities: Spontaneous Activities: Key Achievement:

Nappy Change or Toilet Visits	Time: Wet ☐ Soiled ☐	Time: Wet ☐ Soiled ☐	Time: Wet ☐ Soiled ☐	Time: Wet ☐ Soiled ☐

BOTTLES	Time	Duration	SLEEPS	From	To

○ Breakfast   ○ Lunch   ○ Teatime   ○ Snacks

Parent / Carer Communication:

LINKS TO EYFS	What I Enjoyed Doing Today - Date:

LINKS TO EYFS

- [ ] Self-Regulation
- [ ] Managing Self
- [ ] Building Relationships
- [ ] Listening, Attention and Understanding
- [ ] Speaking
- [ ] Gross Motor Skills
- [ ] Fine Motor Skills
- [ ] Comprehension
- [ ] Word Reading
- [ ] Writing
- [ ] Number
- [ ] Numerical Patterns
- [ ] Past and Present
- [ ] People, Culture and Communities
- [ ] The Natural World
- [ ] Creating with Materials
- [ ] Being Imaginative and Expressive

What I Enjoyed Doing Today - Date:

Planned Activities:

Spontaneous Activities:

Key Achievement:

Nappy Change or Toilet Visits

	Time:		Time:		Time:		Time:	
	Wet	Soiled	Wet	Soiled	Wet	Soiled	Wet	Soiled
	[ ]	[ ]	[ ]	[ ]	[ ]	[ ]	[ ]	[ ]

BOTTLES Time   Duration   **SLEEPS**   From   To

○ Breakfast   ○ Lunch   ○ Teatime   ○ Snacks

Parent / Carer Communication:

LINKS TO EYFS

- [ ] Self-Regulation
- [ ] Managing Self
- [ ] Building Relationships
- [ ] Listening, Attention and Understanding
- [ ] Speaking
- [ ] Gross Motor Skills
- [ ] Fine Motor Skills
- [ ] Comprehension
- [ ] Word Reading
- [ ] Writing
- [ ] Number
- [ ] Numerical Patterns
- [ ] Past and Present
- [ ] People, Culture and Communities
- [ ] The Natural World
- [ ] Creating with Materials
- [ ] Being Imaginative and Expressive

What I Enjoyed Doing Today - Date:

Planned Activities:

Spontaneous Activities:

Key Achievement:

Nappy Change or Toilet Visits

Time:		Time:		Time:		Time:	
Wet	Soiled	Wet	Soiled	Wet	Soiled	Wet	Soiled
[ ]	[ ]	[ ]	[ ]	[ ]	[ ]	[ ]	[ ]

BOTLES	Time	Duration	SLEEPS	From	To

○ Breakfast   ○ Lunch   ○ Teatime   ○ Snacks

Parent / Carer Communication:

NKS TO EYFS	What I Enjoyed Doing Today - Date:
] Self-Regulation	Planned Activities:
] Managing Self	
] Building Relationships	
] Listening, Attention and Understanding	
] Speaking	
] Gross Motor Skills	
] Fine Motor Skills	Spontaneous Activities:
] Comprehension	
] Word Reading	
] Writing	
] Number	
] Numerical Patterns	
] Past and Present	
] People, Culture and Communities	
] The Natural World	Key Achievement:
] Creating with Materials	
] Being Imaginative and Expressive	

appy Change Toilet Visits	Time: Wet ☐	Soiled ☐	Time: Wet ☐	Soiled ☐	Time: Wet ☐	Soiled ☐	Time: Wet ☐	Soiled ☐

OTTLES	Time	Duration	**SLEEPS**	From	To

○ Breakfast   ○ Lunch   ○ Teatime   ○ Snacks

rent / Carer Communication:

LINKS TO EYFS	What I Enjoyed Doing Today - Date:
☐ Self-Regulation ☐ Managing Self ☐ Building Relationships ☐ Listening, Attention and Understanding ☐ Speaking ☐ Gross Motor Skills ☐ Fine Motor Skills ☐ Comprehension ☐ Word Reading ☐ Writing ☐ Number ☐ Numerical Patterns ☐ Past and Present ☐ People, Culture and Communities ☐ The Natural World ☐ Creating with Materials ☐ Being Imaginative and Expressive	Planned Activities: Spontaneous Activities: Key Achievement:

Nappy Change or Toilet Visits	Time: Wet ☐	Soiled ☐	Time: Wet ☐	Soiled ☐	Time: Wet ☐	Soiled ☐	Time: Wet ☐	Soil ☐

BOTTLES	Time	Duration	**SLEEPS**	From	To

○ Breakfast	○ Lunch	○ Teatime	○ Snacks

Parent / Carer Communication:

LINKS TO EYFS

- [ ] Self-Regulation
- [ ] Managing Self
- [ ] Building Relationships
- [ ] Listening, Attention and Understanding
- [ ] Speaking
- [ ] Gross Motor Skills
- [ ] Fine Motor Skills
- [ ] Comprehension
- [ ] Word Reading
- [ ] Writing
- [ ] Number
- [ ] Numerical Patterns
- [ ] Past and Present
- [ ] People, Culture and Communities
- [ ] The Natural World
- [ ] Creating with Materials
- [ ] Being Imaginative and Expressive

What I Enjoyed Doing Today - Date:

Planned Activities:

Spontaneous Activities:

Key Achievement:

Nappy Change or Toilet Visits	Time:		Time:		Time:		Time:	
	Wet	Soiled	Wet	Soiled	Wet	Soiled	Wet	Soiled
	[ ]	[ ]	[ ]	[ ]	[ ]	[ ]	[ ]	[ ]

BOTTLES	Time	Duration	SLEEPS	From	To

Breakfast   Lunch   Teatime   Snacks

Parent / Carer Communication:

LINKS TO EYFS

☐	Self-Regulation
☐	Managing Self
☐	Building Relationships
☐	Listening, Attention and Understanding
☐	Speaking
☐	Gross Motor Skills
☐	Fine Motor Skills
☐	Comprehension
☐	Word Reading
☐	Writing
☐	Number
☐	Numerical Patterns
☐	Past and Present
☐	People, Culture and Communities
☐	The Natural World
☐	Creating with Materials
☐	Being Imaginative and Expressive

What I Enjoyed Doing Today - Date:

Planned Activities:

Spontaneous Activities:

Key Achievement:

Nappy Change or Toilet Visits

Time:		Time:		Time:		Time:	
Wet	Soiled	Wet	Soiled	Wet	Soiled	Wet	Soiled
☐	☐	☐	☐	☐	☐	☐	☐

BOTTLES   Time   Duration   **SLEEPS**   From   To

○ Breakfast   ○ Lunch   ○ Teatime   ○ Snacks

Parent / Carer Communication:

LINKS TO EYFS	What I Enjoyed Doing Today - Date:
☐ Self-Regulation ☐ Managing Self ☐ Building Relationships ☐ Listening, Attention and Understanding ☐ Speaking ☐ Gross Motor Skills ☐ Fine Motor Skills ☐ Comprehension ☐ Word Reading ☐ Writing ☐ Number ☐ Numerical Patterns ☐ Past and Present ☐ People, Culture and Communities ☐ The Natural World ☐ Creating with Materials ☐ Being Imaginative and Expressive	Planned Activities: Spontaneous Activities: Key Achievement:

Nappy Change or Toilet Visits	Time:		Time:		Time:		Time:	
	Wet	Soiled	Wet	Soiled	Wet	Soiled	Wet	Soiled
	☐	☐	☐	☐	☐	☐	☐	☐

BOTTLES	Time	Duration	SLEEPS	From	To

◇ Breakfast   ◇ Lunch   ◇ Teatime   ◇ Snacks

Parent / Carer Communication:

LINKS TO EYFS	What I Enjoyed Doing Today - Date:
☐ Self-Regulation ☐ Managing Self ☐ Building Relationships ☐ Listening, Attention and Understanding ☐ Speaking ☐ Gross Motor Skills ☐ Fine Motor Skills ☐ Comprehension ☐ Word Reading ☐ Writing ☐ Number ☐ Numerical Patterns ☐ Past and Present ☐ People, Culture and Communities ☐ The Natural World ☐ Creating with Materials ☐ Being Imaginative and Expressive	Planned Activities: Spontaneous Activities: Key Achievement:

Nappy Change or Toilet Visits	Time: Wet ☐	Soiled ☐	Time: Wet ☐	Soiled ☐	Time: Wet ☐	Soiled ☐	Time: Wet ☐	Soiled ☐

BOTTLES	Time	Duration	SLEEPS	From	To

○ Breakfast   ○ Lunch   ○ Teatime   ○ Snacks

Parent / Carer Communication:

NKS TO EYFS	What I Enjoyed Doing Today - Date:
Self-Regulation	Planned Activities:
Managing Self	
Building Relationships	
Listening, Attention and Understanding	
Speaking	
Gross Motor Skills	
Fine Motor Skills	Spontaneous Activities:
Comprehension	
Word Reading	
Writing	
Number	
Numerical Patterns	
Past and Present	
People, Culture and Communities	
The Natural World	Key Achievement:
Creating with Materials	
Being Imaginative and Expressive	

appy Change	Time:		Time:		Time:		Time:	
	Wet	Soiled	Wet	Soiled	Wet	Soiled	Wet	Soiled
Toilet Visits	☐	☐	☐	☐	☐	☐	☐	☐

OTTLES	Time	Duration	SLEEPS	From	To

Breakfast   Lunch   Teatime   Snacks

rent / Carer Communication:

LINKS TO EYFS	What I Enjoyed Doing Today - Date:
☐ Self-Regulation ☐ Managing Self ☐ Building Relationships ☐ Listening, Attention and Understanding ☐ Speaking ☐ Gross Motor Skills ☐ Fine Motor Skills ☐ Comprehension ☐ Word Reading ☐ Writing ☐ Number ☐ Numerical Patterns ☐ Past and Present ☐ People, Culture and Communities ☐ The Natural World ☐ Creating with Materials ☐ Being Imaginative and Expressive	Planned Activities: Spontaneous Activities: Key Achievement:

Nappy Change or Toilet Visits	Time: Wet ☐	Soiled ☐	Time: Wet ☐	Soiled ☐	Time: Wet ☐	Soiled ☐	Time: Wet ☐	Soi ☐

BOTTLES	Time	Duration	SLEEPS	From	To

○ Breakfast   ○ Lunch   ○ Teatime   ○ Snacks

Parent / Carer Communication:

LINKS TO EYFS	What I Enjoyed Doing Today - Date:

☐ Self-Regulation
☐ Managing Self
☐ Building Relationships
☐ Listening, Attention
   and Understanding
☐ Speaking
☐ Gross Motor Skills
☐ Fine Motor Skills
☐ Comprehension
☐ Word Reading
☐ Writing
☐ Number
☐ Numerical Patterns
☐ Past and Present
☐ People, Culture and
   Communities
☐ The Natural World
☐ Creating with Materials
☐ Being Imaginative and
   Expressive
	Planned Activities:
	
	Spontaneous Activities:
	
	Key Achievement:

Nappy Change or Toilet Visits	Time: Wet ☐	Soiled ☐	Time: Wet ☐	Soiled ☐	Time: Wet ☐	Soiled ☐	Time: Wet ☐	Soiled ☐

BOTTLES	Time	Duration	SLEEPS	From	To

○ Breakfast   ○ Lunch   ○ Teatime   ○ Snacks

Parent / Carer Communication:

LINKS TO EYFS

- [ ] Self-Regulation
- [ ] Managing Self
- [ ] Building Relationships
- [ ] Listening, Attention and Understanding
- [ ] Speaking
- [ ] Gross Motor Skills
- [ ] Fine Motor Skills
- [ ] Comprehension
- [ ] Word Reading
- [ ] Writing
- [ ] Number
- [ ] Numerical Patterns
- [ ] Past and Present
- [ ] People, Culture and Communities
- [ ] The Natural World
- [ ] Creating with Materials
- [ ] Being Imaginative and Expressive

What I Enjoyed Doing Today - Date:

Planned Activities:

Spontaneous Activities:

Key Achievement:

Nappy Change or Toilet Visits	Time:		Time:		Time:		Time:	
	Wet	Soiled	Wet	Soiled	Wet	Soiled	Wet	Soiled
	[ ]	[ ]	[ ]	[ ]	[ ]	[ ]	[ ]	[ ]

BOTTLES	Time	Duration	SLEEPS	From	To

Breakfast   Lunch   Teatime   Snacks

Parent / Carer Communication:

LINKS TO EYFS	What I Enjoyed Doing Today - Date:
☐ Self-Regulation	Planned Activities:
☐ Managing Self	
☐ Building Relationships	
☐ Listening, Attention and Understanding	
☐ Speaking	
☐ Gross Motor Skills	
☐ Fine Motor Skills	Spontaneous Activities:
☐ Comprehension	
☐ Word Reading	
☐ Writing	
☐ Number	
☐ Numerical Patterns	
☐ Past and Present	
☐ People, Culture and Communities	
☐ The Natural World	Key Achievement:
☐ Creating with Materials	
☐ Being Imaginative and Expressive	

Nappy Change or Toilet Visits	Time:		Time:		Time:		Time:	
	Wet ☐	Soiled ☐	Wet ☐	Soiled ☐	Wet ☐	Soiled ☐	Wet ☐	Soiled ☐

BOTTLES	Time	Duration	SLEEPS	From	To

○ Breakfast   ○ Lunch   ○ Teatime   ○ Snacks

Parent / Carer Communication:

LINKS TO EYFS

- [ ] Self-Regulation
- [ ] Managing Self
- [ ] Building Relationships
- [ ] Listening, Attention and Understanding
- [ ] Speaking
- [ ] Gross Motor Skills
- [ ] Fine Motor Skills
- [ ] Comprehension
- [ ] Word Reading
- [ ] Writing
- [ ] Number
- [ ] Numerical Patterns
- [ ] Past and Present
- [ ] People, Culture and Communities
- [ ] The Natural World
- [ ] Creating with Materials
- [ ] Being Imaginative and Expressive

What I Enjoyed Doing Today - Date:

Planned Activities:

Spontaneous Activities:

Key Achievement:

Nappy Change or Toilet Visits	Time: Wet	Soiled	Time: Wet	Soiled	Time: Wet	Soiled	Time: Wet	Soiled
	[ ]	[ ]	[ ]	[ ]	[ ]	[ ]	[ ]	[ ]

BOTTLES	Time	Duration	SLEEPS	From	To

Breakfast	Lunch	Teatime	Snacks

Parent / Carer Communication:

NKS TO EYFS

] Self-Regulation
] Managing Self
] Building Relationships
] Listening, Attention
  and Understanding
] Speaking
] Gross Motor Skills
] Fine Motor Skills
] Comprehension
] Word Reading
] Writing
] Number
] Numerical Patterns
] Past and Present
] People, Culture and
  Communities
] The Natural World
] Creating with Materials
] Being Imaginative and
  Expressive

What I Enjoyed Doing Today - Date:

Planned Activities:

Spontaneous Activities:

Key Achievement:

appy Change	Time:		Time:		Time:		Time:	
	Wet	Soiled	Wet	Soiled	Wet	Soiled	Wet	Soiled
Toilet Visits	☐	☐	☐	☐	☐	☐	☐	☐

OTTLES	Time	Duration	SLEEPS	From	To

○ Breakfast	○ Lunch	○ Teatime	○ Snacks

arent / Carer Communication:

LINKS TO EYFS	What I Enjoyed Doing Today - Date:
☐ Self-Regulation	Planned Activities:
☐ Managing Self	
☐ Building Relationships	
☐ Listening, Attention and Understanding	
☐ Speaking	
☐ Gross Motor Skills	
☐ Fine Motor Skills	Spontaneous Activities:
☐ Comprehension	
☐ Word Reading	
☐ Writing	
☐ Number	
☐ Numerical Patterns	
☐ Past and Present	
☐ People, Culture and Communities	
☐ The Natural World	Key Achievement:
☐ Creating with Materials	
☐ Being Imaginative and Expressive	

Nappy Change or Toilet Visits	Time:		Time:		Time:		Time:	
	Wet	Soiled	Wet	Soiled	Wet	Soiled	Wet	Soil
	☐	☐	☐	☐	☐	☐	☐	☐

BOTTLES	Time	Duration	SLEEPS	From	To

○ Breakfast	○ Lunch	○ Teatime	○ Snacks

Parent / Carer Communication:

LINKS TO EYFS	What I Enjoyed Doing Today - Date:
☐ Self-Regulation ☐ Managing Self ☐ Building Relationships ☐ Listening, Attention and Understanding ☐ Speaking ☐ Gross Motor Skills ☐ Fine Motor Skills ☐ Comprehension ☐ Word Reading ☐ Writing ☐ Number ☐ Numerical Patterns ☐ Past and Present ☐ People, Culture and Communities ☐ The Natural World ☐ Creating with Materials ☐ Being Imaginative and Expressive	Planned Activities: Spontaneous Activities: Key Achievement:

Nappy Change or Toilet Visits

Time:		Time:		Time:		Time:	
Wet	Soiled	Wet	Soiled	Wet	Soiled	Wet	Soiled
☐	☐	☐	☐	☐	☐	☐	☐

BOTTLES   Time   Duration   **SLEEPS**   From   To

ᵒ Breakfast   ᵒ Lunch   ᵒ Teatime   ᵒ Snacks

Parent / Carer Communication:

LINKS TO EYFS

- ☐ Self-Regulation
- ☐ Managing Self
- ☐ Building Relationships
- ☐ Listening, Attention and Understanding
- ☐ Speaking
- ☐ Gross Motor Skills
- ☐ Fine Motor Skills
- ☐ Comprehension
- ☐ Word Reading
- ☐ Writing
- ☐ Number
- ☐ Numerical Patterns
- ☐ Past and Present
- ☐ People, Culture and Communities
- ☐ The Natural World
- ☐ Creating with Materials
- ☐ Being Imaginative and Expressive

What I Enjoyed Doing Today - Date:

Planned Activities:

Spontaneous Activities:

Key Achievement:

Nappy Change or Toilet Visits	Time:		Time:		Time:		Time:	
	Wet	Soiled	Wet	Soiled	Wet	Soiled	Wet	Soiled
	☐	☐	☐	☐	☐	☐	☐	☐

BOTTLES	Time	Duration	SLEEPS	From	To

Breakfast   Lunch   Teatime   Snacks

Parent / Carer Communication:

LINKS TO EYFS

- ☐ Self-Regulation
- ☐ Managing Self
- ☐ Building Relationships
- ☐ Listening, Attention and Understanding
- ☐ Speaking
- ☐ Gross Motor Skills
- ☐ Fine Motor Skills
- ☐ Comprehension
- ☐ Word Reading
- ☐ Writing
- ☐ Number
- ☐ Numerical Patterns
- ☐ Past and Present
- ☐ People, Culture and Communities
- ☐ The Natural World
- ☐ Creating with Materials
- ☐ Being Imaginative and Expressive

What I Enjoyed Doing Today - Date:

Planned Activities:

Spontaneous Activities:

Key Achievement:

Nappy Change or Toilet Visits	Time:		Time:		Time:		Time:	
	Wet	Soiled	Wet	Soiled	Wet	Soiled	Wet	Soiled
	☐	☐	☐	☐	☐	☐	☐	☐

BOTTLES	Time	Duration	**SLEEPS**	From	To

○ Breakfast   ○ Lunch   ○ Teatime   ○ Snacks

Parent / Carer Communication:

LINKS TO EYFS

- ☐ Self-Regulation
- ☐ Managing Self
- ☐ Building Relationships
- ☐ Listening, Attention and Understanding
- ☐ Speaking
- ☐ Gross Motor Skills
- ☐ Fine Motor Skills
- ☐ Comprehension
- ☐ Word Reading
- ☐ Writing
- ☐ Number
- ☐ Numerical Patterns
- ☐ Past and Present
- ☐ People, Culture and Communities
- ☐ The Natural World
- ☐ Creating with Materials
- ☐ Being Imaginative and Expressive

What I Enjoyed Doing Today - Date:

Planned Activities:

Spontaneous Activities:

Key Achievement:

Nappy Change or Toilet Visits	Time:		Time:		Time:		Time:	
	Wet	Soiled	Wet	Soiled	Wet	Soiled	Wet	Soiled
	☐	☐	☐	☐	☐	☐	☐	☐

BOTTLES	Time	Duration	SLEEPS	From	To

Breakfast   Lunch   Teatime   Snacks

Parent / Carer Communication:

LINKS TO EYFS

- [ ] Self-Regulation
- [ ] Managing Self
- [ ] Building Relationships
- [ ] Listening, Attention and Understanding
- [ ] Speaking
- [ ] Gross Motor Skills
- [ ] Fine Motor Skills
- [ ] Comprehension
- [ ] Word Reading
- [ ] Writing
- [ ] Number
- [ ] Numerical Patterns
- [ ] Past and Present
- [ ] People, Culture and Communities
- [ ] The Natural World
- [ ] Creating with Materials
- [ ] Being Imaginative and Expressive

What I Enjoyed Doing Today - Date:

Planned Activities:

Spontaneous Activities:

Key Achievement:

Nappy Change Toilet Visits	Time:		Time:		Time:		Time:	
	Wet	Soiled	Wet	Soiled	Wet	Soiled	Wet	Soiled
	☐	☐	☐	☐	☐	☐	☐	☐

BOTTLES	Time	Duration	SLEEPS	From	To

Breakfast Lunch Teatime Snacks

Parent / Carer Communication:

LINKS TO EYFS

- ☐ Self-Regulation
- ☐ Managing Self
- ☐ Building Relationships
- ☐ Listening, Attention and Understanding
- ☐ Speaking
- ☐ Gross Motor Skills
- ☐ Fine Motor Skills
- ☐ Comprehension
- ☐ Word Reading
- ☐ Writing
- ☐ Number
- ☐ Numerical Patterns
- ☐ Past and Present
- ☐ People, Culture and Communities
- ☐ The Natural World
- ☐ Creating with Materials
- ☐ Being Imaginative and Expressive

What I Enjoyed Doing Today - Date:

Planned Activities:

Spontaneous Activities:

Key Achievement:

Nappy Change or Toilet Visits	Time:		Time:		Time:		Time:	
	Wet	Soiled	Wet	Soiled	Wet	Soiled	Wet	Soil
	☐	☐	☐	☐	☐	☐	☐	☐

BOTTLES	Time	Duration	SLEEPS	From	To

ᵒ Breakfast   ᵒ Lunch   ᵒ Teatime   ᵒ Snacks

Parent / Carer Communication:

LINKS TO EYFS	What I Enjoyed Doing Today - Date:
☐ Self-Regulation ☐ Managing Self ☐ Building Relationships ☐ Listening, Attention and Understanding ☐ Speaking ☐ Gross Motor Skills ☐ Fine Motor Skills ☐ Comprehension ☐ Word Reading ☐ Writing ☐ Number ☐ Numerical Patterns ☐ Past and Present ☐ People, Culture and Communities ☐ The Natural World ☐ Creating with Materials ☐ Being Imaginative and Expressive	Planned Activities: Spontaneous Activities: Key Achievement:

Nappy Change or Toilet Visits	Time:		Time:		Time:		Time:	
	Wet	Soiled	Wet	Soiled	Wet	Soiled	Wet	Soiled
	☐	☐	☐	☐	☐	☐	☐	☐

BOTTLES	Time	Duration	SLEEPS	From	To

○ Breakfast   ○ Lunch   ○ Teatime   ○ Snacks

Parent / Carer Communication:

LINKS TO EYFS

- [ ] Self-Regulation
- [ ] Managing Self
- [ ] Building Relationships
- [ ] Listening, Attention and Understanding
- [ ] Speaking
- [ ] Gross Motor Skills
- [ ] Fine Motor Skills
- [ ] Comprehension
- [ ] Word Reading
- [ ] Writing
- [ ] Number
- [ ] Numerical Patterns
- [ ] Past and Present
- [ ] People, Culture and Communities
- [ ] The Natural World
- [ ] Creating with Materials
- [ ] Being Imaginative and Expressive

What I Enjoyed Doing Today - Date:

Planned Activities:

Spontaneous Activities:

Key Achievement:

Nappy Change or Toilet Visits	Time:		Time:		Time:		Time:	
	Wet	Soiled	Wet	Soiled	Wet	Soiled	Wet	Soiled
	☐	☐	☐	☐	☐	☐	☐	☐

BOTTLES	Time	Duration	SLEEPS	From	To

○ Breakfast ○ Lunch ○ Teatime ○ Snacks

Parent / Carer Communication:

LINKS TO EYFS

- [ ] Self-Regulation
- [ ] Managing Self
- [ ] Building Relationships
- [ ] Listening, Attention and Understanding
- [ ] Speaking
- [ ] Gross Motor Skills
- [ ] Fine Motor Skills
- [ ] Comprehension
- [ ] Word Reading
- [ ] Writing
- [ ] Number
- [ ] Numerical Patterns
- [ ] Past and Present
- [ ] People, Culture and Communities
- [ ] The Natural World
- [ ] Creating with Materials
- [ ] Being Imaginative and Expressive

What I Enjoyed Doing Today - Date:

Planned Activities:

Spontaneous Activities:

Key Achievement:

Nappy Change or Toilet Visits	Time:		Time:		Time:		Time:	
	Wet	Soiled	Wet	Soiled	Wet	Soiled	Wet	Soiled
	[ ]	[ ]	[ ]	[ ]	[ ]	[ ]	[ ]	[ ]

BOTTLES Time Duration **SLEEPS** From To

Breakfast   Lunch   Teatime   Snacks

Parent / Carer Communication:

LINKS TO EYFS

- ☐ Self-Regulation
- ☐ Managing Self
- ☐ Building Relationships
- ☐ Listening, Attention and Understanding
- ☐ Speaking
- ☐ Gross Motor Skills
- ☐ Fine Motor Skills
- ☐ Comprehension
- ☐ Word Reading
- ☐ Writing
- ☐ Number
- ☐ Numerical Patterns
- ☐ Past and Present
- ☐ People, Culture and Communities
- ☐ The Natural World
- ☐ Creating with Materials
- ☐ Being Imaginative and Expressive

What I Enjoyed Doing Today - Date:

Planned Activities:

Spontaneous Activities:

Key Achievement:

Nappy Change or Toilet Visits	Time:		Time:		Time:		Time:	
	Wet	Soiled	Wet	Soiled	Wet	Soiled	Wet	Soiled
	☐	☐	☐	☐	☐	☐	☐	☐

BOTTLES	Time	Duration	SLEEPS	From	To

○ Breakfast   ○ Lunch   ○ Teatime   ○ Snacks

Parent / Carer Communication:

NKS TO EYFS

-] Self-Regulation
-] Managing Self
-] Building Relationships
-] Listening, Attention and Understanding
-] Speaking
-] Gross Motor Skills
-] Fine Motor Skills
-] Comprehension
-] Word Reading
-] Writing
-] Number
-] Numerical Patterns
-] Past and Present
-] People, Culture and Communities
-] The Natural World
-] Creating with Materials
-] Being Imaginative and Expressive

What I Enjoyed Doing Today - Date:

Planned Activities:

Spontaneous Activities:

Key Achievement:

appy Change	Time:		Time:		Time:		Time:	
	Wet	Soiled	Wet	Soiled	Wet	Soiled	Wet	Soiled
Toilet Visits	☐	☐	☐	☐	☐	☐	☐	☐

OTTLES	Time	Duration	SLEEPS	From	To

Breakfast   Lunch   Teatime   Snacks

rent / Carer Communication:

LINKS TO EYFS	What I Enjoyed Doing Today - Date:
☐ Self-Regulation ☐ Managing Self ☐ Building Relationships ☐ Listening, Attention 　 and Understanding ☐ Speaking ☐ Gross Motor Skills ☐ Fine Motor Skills ☐ Comprehension ☐ Word Reading ☐ Writing ☐ Number ☐ Numerical Patterns ☐ Past and Present ☐ People, Culture and 　 Communities ☐ The Natural World ☐ Creating with Materials ☐ Being Imaginative and 　 Expressive	Planned Activities: Spontaneous Activities: Key Achievement:

Nappy Change or Toilet Visits	Time: Wet ☐	Soiled ☐	Time: Wet ☐	Soiled ☐	Time: Wet ☐	Soiled ☐	Time: Wet ☐	Soil ☐

BOTTLES	Time	Duration	SLEEPS	From	To

○ Breakfast　　　○ Lunch　　　　○ Teatime　　　　○ Snacks

Parent / Carer Communication:

LINKS TO EYFS	What I Enjoyed Doing Today - Date:

☐ Self-Regulation
☐ Managing Self
☐ Building Relationships
☐ Listening, Attention
  and Understanding
☐ Speaking
☐ Gross Motor Skills
☐ Fine Motor Skills
☐ Comprehension
☐ Word Reading
☐ Writing
☐ Number
☐ Numerical Patterns
☐ Past and Present
☐ People, Culture and
  Communities
☐ The Natural World
☐ Creating with Materials
☐ Being Imaginative and
  Expressive
	Planned Activities:
	
	Spontaneous Activities:
	
	Key Achievement:

Nappy Change or Toilet Visits	Time:		Time:		Time:		Time:	
	Wet	Soiled	Wet	Soiled	Wet	Soiled	Wet	Soiled
	☐	☐	☐	☐	☐	☐	☐	☐

BOTTLES	Time	Duration	SLEEPS	From	To

Breakfast   Lunch   Teatime   Snacks

Parent / Carer Communication:

LINKS TO EYFS

- [ ] Self-Regulation
- [ ] Managing Self
- [ ] Building Relationships
- [ ] Listening, Attention and Understanding
- [ ] Speaking
- [ ] Gross Motor Skills
- [ ] Fine Motor Skills
- [ ] Comprehension
- [ ] Word Reading
- [ ] Writing
- [ ] Number
- [ ] Numerical Patterns
- [ ] Past and Present
- [ ] People, Culture and Communities
- [ ] The Natural World
- [ ] Creating with Materials
- [ ] Being Imaginative and Expressive

What I Enjoyed Doing Today - Date:

Planned Activities:

Spontaneous Activities:

Key Achievement:

Nappy Change or Toilet Visits	Time:		Time:		Time:		Time:	
	Wet	Soiled	Wet	Soiled	Wet	Soiled	Wet	Soiled
	[ ]	[ ]	[ ]	[ ]	[ ]	[ ]	[ ]	[ ]

BOTTLES	Time	Duration	SLEEPS	From	To

Breakfast   Lunch   Teatime   Snacks

Parent / Carer Communication:

LINKS TO EYFS

| | What I Enjoyed Doing Today - Date: |

- ☐ Self-Regulation
- ☐ Managing Self
- ☐ Building Relationships
- ☐ Listening, Attention and Understanding
- ☐ Speaking
- ☐ Gross Motor Skills
- ☐ Fine Motor Skills
- ☐ Comprehension
- ☐ Word Reading
- ☐ Writing
- ☐ Number
- ☐ Numerical Patterns
- ☐ Past and Present
- ☐ People, Culture and Communities
- ☐ The Natural World
- ☐ Creating with Materials
- ☐ Being Imaginative and Expressive

Planned Activities:

Spontaneous Activities:

Key Achievement:

Nappy Change or Toilet Visits	Time:		Time:		Time:		Time:	
	Wet	Soiled	Wet	Soiled	Wet	Soiled	Wet	Soiled
	☐	☐	☐	☐	☐	☐	☐	☐

BOTTLES	Time	Duration	**SLEEPS**	From	To

⚬ Breakfast　　⚬ Lunch　　⚬ Teatime　　⚬ Snacks

Parent / Carer Communication:

LINKS TO EYFS

- [ ] Self-Regulation
- [ ] Managing Self
- [ ] Building Relationships
- [ ] Listening, Attention and Understanding
- [ ] Speaking
- [ ] Gross Motor Skills
- [ ] Fine Motor Skills
- [ ] Comprehension
- [ ] Word Reading
- [ ] Writing
- [ ] Number
- [ ] Numerical Patterns
- [ ] Past and Present
- [ ] People, Culture and Communities
- [ ] The Natural World
- [ ] Creating with Materials
- [ ] Being Imaginative and Expressive

What I Enjoyed Doing Today - Date:

Planned Activities:

Spontaneous Activities:

Key Achievement:

Nappy Change or Toilet Visits	Time:		Time:		Time:		Time:	
	Wet	Soiled	Wet	Soiled	Wet	Soiled	Wet	Soiled
	[ ]	[ ]	[ ]	[ ]	[ ]	[ ]	[ ]	[ ]

BOTTLES	Time	Duration	SLEEPS	From	To

Breakfast   Lunch   Teatime   Snacks

Parent / Carer Communication:

LINKS TO EYFS

- [ ] Self-Regulation
- [ ] Managing Self
- [ ] Building Relationships
- [ ] Listening, Attention and Understanding
- [ ] Speaking
- [ ] Gross Motor Skills
- [ ] Fine Motor Skills
- [ ] Comprehension
- [ ] Word Reading
- [ ] Writing
- [ ] Number
- [ ] Numerical Patterns
- [ ] Past and Present
- [ ] People, Culture and Communities
- [ ] The Natural World
- [ ] Creating with Materials
- [ ] Being Imaginative and Expressive

What I Enjoyed Doing Today - Date:

Planned Activities:

Spontaneous Activities:

Key Achievement:

Nappy Change / Toilet Visits

Time:		Time:		Time:		Time:	
Wet	Soiled	Wet	Soiled	Wet	Soiled	Wet	Soiled
☐	☐	☐	☐	☐	☐	☐	☐

BOTTLES	Time	Duration	SLEEPS	From	To

Breakfast   Lunch   Teatime   Snacks

Parent / Carer Communication:

LINKS TO EYFS	What I Enjoyed Doing Today - Date:
☐ Self-Regulation	Planned Activities:
☐ Managing Self	
☐ Building Relationships	
☐ Listening, Attention and Understanding	
☐ Speaking	
☐ Gross Motor Skills	
☐ Fine Motor Skills	Spontaneous Activities:
☐ Comprehension	
☐ Word Reading	
☐ Writing	
☐ Number	
☐ Numerical Patterns	
☐ Past and Present	
☐ People, Culture and Communities	
☐ The Natural World	Key Achievement:
☐ Creating with Materials	
☐ Being Imaginative and Expressive	

Nappy Change or Toilet Visits	Time:		Time:		Time:		Time:	
	Wet ☐	Soiled ☐	Wet ☐	Soiled ☐	Wet ☐	Soiled ☐	Wet ☐	Soil☐

BOTTLES	Time	Duration	SLEEPS	From	To

Breakfast	Lunch	Teatime	Snacks

Parent / Carer Communication:

LINKS TO EYFS	What I Enjoyed Doing Today - Date:
☐ Self-Regulation ☐ Managing Self ☐ Building Relationships ☐ Listening, Attention and Understanding ☐ Speaking ☐ Gross Motor Skills ☐ Fine Motor Skills ☐ Comprehension ☐ Word Reading ☐ Writing ☐ Number ☐ Numerical Patterns ☐ Past and Present ☐ People, Culture and Communities ☐ The Natural World ☐ Creating with Materials ☐ Being Imaginative and Expressive	Planned Activities: Spontaneous Activities: Key Achievement:

Nappy Change or Toilet Visits

	Time:		Time:		Time:		Time:	
	Wet	Soiled	Wet	Soiled	Wet	Soiled	Wet	Soiled
	☐	☐	☐	☐	☐	☐	☐	☐

BOTTLES	Time	Duration	**SLEEPS**	From	To

○ Breakfast   ○ Lunch   ○ Teatime   ○ Snacks

Parent / Carer Communication:

LINKS TO EYFS

- [ ] Self-Regulation
- [ ] Managing Self
- [ ] Building Relationships
- [ ] Listening, Attention and Understanding
- [ ] Speaking
- [ ] Gross Motor Skills
- [ ] Fine Motor Skills
- [ ] Comprehension
- [ ] Word Reading
- [ ] Writing
- [ ] Number
- [ ] Numerical Patterns
- [ ] Past and Present
- [ ] People, Culture and Communities
- [ ] The Natural World
- [ ] Creating with Materials
- [ ] Being Imaginative and Expressive

What I Enjoyed Doing Today - Date:

Planned Activities:

Spontaneous Activities:

Key Achievement:

Nappy Change or Toilet Visits	Time:		Time:		Time:		Time:	
	Wet	Soiled	Wet	Soiled	Wet	Soiled	Wet	Soiled
	[ ]	[ ]	[ ]	[ ]	[ ]	[ ]	[ ]	[ ]

BOTTLES	Time	Duration	SLEEPS	From	To

Breakfast   Lunch   Teatime   Snacks

Parent / Carer Communication:

LINKS TO EYFS	What I Enjoyed Doing Today - Date:
☐ Self-Regulation	Planned Activities:
☐ Managing Self	
☐ Building Relationships	
☐ Listening, Attention and Understanding	
☐ Speaking	
☐ Gross Motor Skills	
☐ Fine Motor Skills	Spontaneous Activities:
☐ Comprehension	
☐ Word Reading	
☐ Writing	
☐ Number	
☐ Numerical Patterns	
☐ Past and Present	
☐ People, Culture and Communities	
☐ The Natural World	Key Achievement:
☐ Creating with Materials	
☐ Being Imaginative and Expressive	

Nappy Change or Toilet Visits	Time:		Time:		Time:		Time:	
	Wet	Soiled	Wet	Soiled	Wet	Soiled	Wet	Soiled
	☐	☐	☐	☐	☐	☐	☐	☐

BOTTLES	Time	Duration	SLEEPS	From	To

Breakfast   Lunch   Teatime   Snacks

Parent / Carer Communication:

LINKS TO EYFS

- [ ] Self-Regulation
- [ ] Managing Self
- [ ] Building Relationships
- [ ] Listening, Attention and Understanding
- [ ] Speaking
- [ ] Gross Motor Skills
- [ ] Fine Motor Skills
- [ ] Comprehension
- [ ] Word Reading
- [ ] Writing
- [ ] Number
- [ ] Numerical Patterns
- [ ] Past and Present
- [ ] People, Culture and Communities
- [ ] The Natural World
- [ ] Creating with Materials
- [ ] Being Imaginative and Expressive

What I Enjoyed Doing Today - Date:

Planned Activities:

Spontaneous Activities:

Key Achievement:

Nappy Change or Toilet Visits	Time:		Time:		Time:		Time:	
	Wet	Soiled	Wet	Soiled	Wet	Soiled	Wet	Soiled
	[ ]	[ ]	[ ]	[ ]	[ ]	[ ]	[ ]	[ ]

BOTTLES	Time	Duration	SLEEPS	From	To

Breakfast   Lunch   Teatime   Snacks

Parent / Carer Communication:

LINKS TO EYFS

- Self-Regulation
- Managing Self
- Building Relationships
- Listening, Attention and Understanding
- Speaking
- Gross Motor Skills
- Fine Motor Skills
- Comprehension
- Word Reading
- Writing
- Number
- Numerical Patterns
- Past and Present
- People, Culture and Communities
- The Natural World
- Creating with Materials
- Being Imaginative and Expressive

What I Enjoyed Doing Today - Date:

Planned Activities:

Spontaneous Activities:

Key Achievement:

Nappy Change / Toilet Visits	Time:		Time:		Time:		Time:	
	Wet	Soiled	Wet	Soiled	Wet	Soiled	Wet	Soiled
	☐	☐	☐	☐	☐	☐	☐	☐

BOTTLES	Time	Duration	SLEEPS	From	To

Breakfast   Lunch   Teatime   Snacks

Parent / Carer Communication:

LINKS TO EYFS	What I Enjoyed Doing Today - Date:
☐ Self-Regulation ☐ Managing Self ☐ Building Relationships ☐ Listening, Attention and Understanding ☐ Speaking ☐ Gross Motor Skills ☐ Fine Motor Skills ☐ Comprehension ☐ Word Reading ☐ Writing ☐ Number ☐ Numerical Patterns ☐ Past and Present ☐ People, Culture and Communities ☐ The Natural World ☐ Creating with Materials ☐ Being Imaginative and Expressive	Planned Activities: Spontaneous Activities: Key Achievement:

Nappy Change or Toilet Visits	Time: Wet ☐	Soiled ☐	Time: Wet ☐	Soiled ☐	Time: Wet ☐	Soiled ☐	Time: Wet ☐	Soil ☐

BOTTLES	Time	Duration	**SLEEPS**	From	To

○ Breakfast	○ Lunch	○ Teatime	○ Snacks

Parent / Carer Communication:

LINKS TO EYFS

- ☐ Self-Regulation
- ☐ Managing Self
- ☐ Building Relationships
- ☐ Listening, Attention and Understanding
- ☐ Speaking
- ☐ Gross Motor Skills
- ☐ Fine Motor Skills
- ☐ Comprehension
- ☐ Word Reading
- ☐ Writing
- ☐ Number
- ☐ Numerical Patterns
- ☐ Past and Present
- ☐ People, Culture and Communities
- ☐ The Natural World
- ☐ Creating with Materials
- ☐ Being Imaginative and Expressive

What I Enjoyed Doing Today - Date:

Planned Activities:

Spontaneous Activities:

Key Achievement:

Nappy Change or Toilet Visits	Time:		Time:		Time:		Time:	
	Wet	Soiled	Wet	Soiled	Wet	Soiled	Wet	Soiled
	☐	☐	☐	☐	☐	☐	☐	☐

BOTTLES	Time	Duration	SLEEPS	From	To

- ○ Breakfast
- ○ Lunch
- ○ Teatime
- ○ Snacks

Parent / Carer Communication:

LINKS TO EYFS	What I Enjoyed Doing Today - Date:
☐ Self-Regulation ☐ Managing Self ☐ Building Relationships ☐ Listening, Attention and Understanding ☐ Speaking ☐ Gross Motor Skills ☐ Fine Motor Skills ☐ Comprehension ☐ Word Reading ☐ Writing ☐ Number ☐ Numerical Patterns ☐ Past and Present ☐ People, Culture and Communities ☐ The Natural World ☐ Creating with Materials ☐ Being Imaginative and Expressive	Planned Activities: Spontaneous Activities: Key Achievement:

Nappy Change or Toilet Visits	Time:		Time:		Time:		Time:	
	Wet ☐	Soiled ☐	Wet ☐	Soiled ☐	Wet ☐	Soiled ☐	Wet ☐	Soiled ☐

BOTTLES	Time	Duration	SLEEPS	From	To

○ Breakfast   ○ Lunch   ○ Teatime   ○ Snacks

Parent / Carer Communication:

LINKS TO EYFS

- ☐ Self-Regulation
- ☐ Managing Self
- ☐ Building Relationships
- ☐ Listening, Attention and Understanding
- ☐ Speaking
- ☐ Gross Motor Skills
- ☐ Fine Motor Skills
- ☐ Comprehension
- ☐ Word Reading
- ☐ Writing
- ☐ Number
- ☐ Numerical Patterns
- ☐ Past and Present
- ☐ People, Culture and Communities
- ☐ The Natural World
- ☐ Creating with Materials
- ☐ Being Imaginative and Expressive

What I Enjoyed Doing Today - Date:

Planned Activities:

Spontaneous Activities:

Key Achievement:

Nappy Change or Toilet Visits	Time:		Time:		Time:		Time:	
	Wet	Soiled	Wet	Soiled	Wet	Soiled	Wet	Soiled
	☐	☐	☐	☐	☐	☐	☐	☐

BOTTLES	Time	Duration	**SLEEPS**	From	To

Breakfast   Lunch   Teatime   Snacks

Parent / Carer Communication:

LINKS TO EYFS	What I Enjoyed Doing Today - Date:

☐ Self-Regulation
☐ Managing Self
☐ Building Relationships
☐ Listening, Attention
  and Understanding
☐ Speaking
☐ Gross Motor Skills
☐ Fine Motor Skills
☐ Comprehension
☐ Word Reading
☐ Writing
☐ Number
☐ Numerical Patterns
☐ Past and Present
☐ People, Culture and
  Communities
☐ The Natural World
☐ Creating with Materials
☐ Being Imaginative and
  Expressive
	Planned Activities:
	
	Spontaneous Activities:
	
	Key Achievement:

Nappy Change or Toilet Visits	Time: Wet ☐	Soiled ☐	Time: Wet ☐	Soiled ☐	Time: Wet ☐	Soiled ☐	Time: Wet ☐	Soiled ☐

BOTTLES	Time	Duration	SLEEPS	From	To

○ Breakfast ○ Lunch ○ Teatime ○ Snacks

Parent / Carer Communication:

LINKS TO EYFS

- [ ] Self-Regulation
- [ ] Managing Self
- [ ] Building Relationships
- [ ] Listening, Attention and Understanding
- [ ] Speaking
- [ ] Gross Motor Skills
- [ ] Fine Motor Skills
- [ ] Comprehension
- [ ] Word Reading
- [ ] Writing
- [ ] Number
- [ ] Numerical Patterns
- [ ] Past and Present
- [ ] People, Culture and Communities
- [ ] The Natural World
- [ ] Creating with Materials
- [ ] Being Imaginative and Expressive

What I Enjoyed Doing Today - Date:

Planned Activities:

Spontaneous Activities:

Key Achievement:

Nappy Change / Toilet Visits

Time:		Time:		Time:		Time:	
Wet	Soiled	Wet	Soiled	Wet	Soiled	Wet	Soiled
☐	☐	☐	☐	☐	☐	☐	☐

BOTTLES	Time	Duration	SLEEPS	From	To

○ Breakfast   ○ Lunch   ○ Teatime   ○ Snacks

Parent / Carer Communication:

MONTHLY PLANNER

Month

01	02	03	04	05	06	
08	09	10	11	12	13	
15	16	17	18	19	20	
22	23	24	25	26	27	
29	30	31	*Delete day (31) were applicable.			

Month

01	02	03	04	05	06	
08	09	10	11	12	13	
15	16	17	18	19	20	
22	23	24	25	26	27	
29	30	31	*Delete day (31) were applicable.			

MONTHLY PLANNER

Month

01	02	03	04	05	06	07
08	09	10	11	12	13	14
15	16	17	18	19	20	21
22	23	24	25	26	27	28
29	30	31	*Delete day (31) were applicable.			

Carers Details

Name

Address

Tel:

Email:

Bespoke Childcare Diaries & Bulk Purchase Discounts.

Standard Diaries
Your cover design / logo * This diary is our standard format.

Ordering Options
Discounted bulk purchase direct from our website - Minimum order 30 Diaries

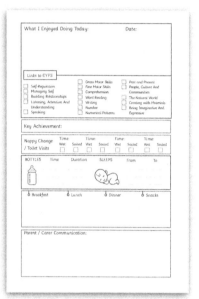

Bespoke Diaries
Your layout, interior design, book size & colour options. * Artwork charges apply

Ordering Options
No minimum order - purchase direct from amazon.

For more information visit our website: www.bound2beperfect.com

Printed in Great Britain
by Amazon

15687114R00058

DREAMING OF AN EMPIRE

THE QUEEN IS THE MOST POWERFUL PIECE IN THE GAME

VIKTORIA MCCORMACK

INTRODUCTION

This book was written during the winter of 2021, it tells the story of struggle, hardship, loss, fights, battles, and eventually success. It was written with the intent to help others realise, that no matter how difficult times may get, we can always come back from the fight. It's the real, raw truth of life. Those that know me as a friend may see success, but behind every success, there is a story that made someone strong enough to face battles that many are unaware of.

I want to share this story, the good, the bad, and the ugly and as a disclaimer, I must emphasise that there may be trigger warnings for some.

Life is hard. We all have a story to tell and by telling mine I pray that it helps one person to never give up their dreams, to never stop working towards what you deserve, and to push through the storm. Please take solitude in the thought that you are not alone on your journey through life, nor are you alone with the experiences you have been through.

COPYRIGHT

I dedicate this book to the most extraordinary woman I have ever known, my beautiful Nanny Jean. It is through her that I am alive today to tell this story and I hope that by writing my story, I can show her my gratitude for all she has done.

Our time together hasn't always been easy, I have put you through things no family member should ever have to go through, but you've always stayed present no matter what. The endless phone calls I made to you when I was scared and the times you picked me up when I was down. Your amazing hugs that heal my soul from a single touch and the safety I feel when your arms are wrapped around me so tightly. I have the utmost respect for you and I owe you my life.

You said one day I would write a book, so here it is, in the only way I know how.

"I love you to the moon, the stars, and back again."

CONTENTS

A NOTE FROM THE AUTHOR

I am a woman from a little place in England called Blackpool with a story that needs to be told. My story isn't over, but it began with struggling, such as many others may have too. I have worked from 13 years old, whether it was in hotels, in telesales, shops, or local authority children's homes. I have been to university and studied health and social care at both foundation and honours degree level. I have also completed my Post Graduate Certificate in Education, which allows me to teach students above the age of 16. I am proud of the journey I have been on. It hasn't all been fun, but this is the reason I wrote this memoir. My story has included pivotal stages in life that could have broken me. I chose to stand against the odds, to help other women like me, that have been through difficult times. I hope, that by reading my journey, you can take away some sense of security that nothing in life is impossible, but also that nothing in life that happens to you, should change who you are meant to be.

My nan told me that one day, I would write a book, so here I am. And though I wrote this for myself in a bid to help myself heal. I also write this for the women (and men) that have been at their lowest and I hope that utilising my voice will allow me to be heard, to help and eventually heal those too.

After starting with nothing, I now have my very own large and successful training academy. We constantly receive five-star reviews from our students and clients across the board and recently we were nominated for 'Training Academy of the Year' 2020. Some of my students have known some of my stories and have inspired me to push forward with this. They tell me that I am inspirational and for me, that means everything. I wish to inspire the world and hope I can do this by connecting with you reading my book.

Due to the nature of this book, I would like to include some helpline websites, where you will find numbers for those that are in need and may need help.

- Women's Aid- Support for victims of and survivors of domestic abuse: www.womensaid.org.uk
- Rape Crisis- Victims and survivors of rape and sexual assault: www.rapecrisis.org.uk
- Salvation Army- Homelessness support: www.salvationarmy.org.uk
- Mind- Mental health/emotional support: www.mind.org.uk
- National Domestic Abuse Helpline: www.nationalahelpline.org.uk
- Survivors Trust- Specialists in rape and sexual abuse services: www.thesurviviorstrust.org
- Male survivors partnership: www.malesurvivor.co.uk
- Mental health/young people: www.youngminds.org.uk
- Victim support for all victims of crime or traumatic events: www.victimsupport.org.uk
- Mental health/ LGBTQ: www.mindout.org.uk
- Refuge- Providing support for victims and survivors of domestic abuse: www.refuge.org.uk

NOWHERE TO GO

My time at the B&B was a huge eye-opener. I was dumped in a room that was damp. I had no money, I couldn't even afford toothpaste, shampoo, or conditioner, let alone be able to wash my clothes. One evening, I had gone back to the area I knew to see some friends, I remember walking eight miles just so I was able to see someone I knew. Of course then I had to walk back as well, I would do this often.

It was around midnight by the time I got home one evening and as I went up to my room, I opened my door and noticed there was a heavyset, dirty older man in my bed, snoring! All my things had been dumped in the hall and I was told by the staff there that I had to leave. When I say all my things most were missing, including the clothes I used and desperately needed for work! I remember being so upset because I had washed my underwear with some soap I found and had left it all drying on the side of the sink (there were no radiators) and it was just thrown in the hall. I explained I had nowhere to go, especially not at this time! They let me stay for a final night then woke me at 6am to leave. I had to again go back to the homeless office and explain, they told me that until I turned 16, they couldn't do anything to help except guide me to the local homeless shelter. I spent one night in there, the other nights I had to find somewhere else to sleep because there was no room left, despite how early I got there, I think they only had ten beds. To be quite honest, it wasn't the nicest of places to be anyway, the only solitude was that I would be able to get something to eat, have a little wash and be safe when I was sleeping. At that moment, I remember feeling so broken, so lost, I felt like a failure. And on top of that, I was still trying to comprehend what had happened. I couldn't keep my job because I couldn't even wash, and I had no uniform or any clothes other than the ones on my back. I tried to find warm places to stay but it was difficult, I wasn't used to the streets and unfortunately as a society we see homeless people as outcasts, people who drink too much or take drugs and then there's those that judge the homeless as if they must have done something awful to be there. I couldn't bring myself to tell my nan, I didn't want to lose that sense of pride she had for me. So I rode it out, sleeping in any quiet places I could find.

I would sit in the freezing cold of the night and watch people as they walked by, they would cross the road to avoid me, they would spit as they walked past me, it was only one occasion where a guy bought me a warm drink. By then I was well and truly wary of men and their intentions, so I took the drink, thanked him, and put my head down. However, I still remember the fear of glancing at him. What if he had other intentions? What if he wanted something in return and do I even take the drink? Even worse, what if it was somebody I knew?

Once I was closer to turning 16, I returned to the homeless office asking for help. Fortunately for me, a lovely woman took pity on me and did what she could to find me a hostel to live in that was close to the area I had been staying in when I was in the B&B. Now, this hostel wasn't exactly The Ritz, it wasn't in the area I knew well but it was somewhere to stay. Finally, I had somewhere I could feel safe. I had finally caught a break!

CUSTARD CREAMS AND CRAB STICKS

From the age of eight years old, I quickly learned that life was not always rainbows and unicorns. I grew up in a household that was rife with violence, arguments, and torment. My mother was raising four children on her own and it was not uncommon for me to see different men in and out of our lives. Being the eldest it was left to me to find a way to survive. My mother had tried, but unfortunately, her taste in men had a lot to be desired. Before this, we had grown up in a heavily impoverished council estate. As a young child, I knew no better, we would stay out until the late hours, running wild, and back then was a time I remember being happy. My mother struggled, we didn't have nice clothes, we didn't have nice food, or much food at all for that matter. We lived hand to mouth. I remember an older man that lived below us in the flats, Uncle Fred I called him (though I didn't know if that were his real name!) he was in a wheelchair and I would sneak down for food... he would give me custard creams and crab sticks and I was so grateful. I often sat in his flat for hours talking to him, he would invite me in when he saw me in the hallway of the rundown flats. With broken windows, no friends to play with, usually still in my pyjamas by the afternoon. I remember his flat, it was warm, a little cluttered, and untidy but it was a safe place for me. It was nicer in comparison to the rundown flat we lived in upstairs, with smashed windows and bare cupboards. It was so cold; you could see your breath when you spoke. Whenever my brother's dad came around, I knew arguments and violence would occur and I quickly made my exit down to my uncle's flat on the bottom floor, shouting through the letterbox and peeking in to see if he was coming as I always did. Unfortunately, one day, that came to an end when I had peeked through the letterbox to see if he was coming to bring me some food and tell me some of his stories, instead I saw him lying on the floor out of his chair. I continued to shout at him and got no response. He was pronounced deceased once the ambulance team arrived. There were no more stories he would tell me from his war days, no more warmth, no more crab sticks and custard creams. I think that's the first memory I remember of feeling lonely and dealing with grief alone. My nan would visit often, and she would take me out to the beach, buy me an ice lolly and take me back to hers for a warm tea, a hot bath, and then drop me back at home. It soon became apparent the love and bond I had with my nan.

My mum, myself and my younger brother Ryan eventually moved to a new council estate, a house this time, but not much of a better area. I never had many friends; the kids were mean and would make fun of the fact that I didn't have nice clothes or toys. I was often bullied by the older children and my mum would end up chasing them down the street like a lioness protecting her cub! I adored my mum back then, times were hard, but she did everything she could to give us what we needed. I just remember having my little brother Ryan at the time, who always used to follow me around annoying me and saying my name wrong "Vicky-tora" he would call me! (In reality, I didn't mind, because I felt less alone) I had a couple of 'friends' but they never really stuck about for long. I relied mostly upon my Aunty Bev and cousin Jade for solitude in family life whenever I could. My Aunty Bev would take us on amazing walks in the countryside and away for weekends. I loved being at her house, it always felt so rich in comparison to our home. Her cooking was the best too! Jade had so many amazing toys, the newest Baby G watch that she would let me wear (for ten minutes before she wanted it back!) but I loved it. We were inseparable. On Saturdays, we would make a trip to Safeway (remember that?) and buy sweets for movie nights and a sleepover. These were happy times. Playing out on the street without a care in the world, lots of friends on what I think we used to call 'The Green', it was a large patch of grass, where all the kids played. One day I remember exploring with Jade and we snuck down the back of the old tram tracks, Jade ended up with a nail straight through her shoe and into her foot. We were more worried about what Aunty Bev would say when we had to tell her how it happened, you could never get away with telling fibs to Aunty Bev, she always just knew! We were forever getting into mischief, but we loved it and were always laughing.

BEING MUM

My mum met a man called Dave when I was eight years old, who soon then became the father to my younger siblings David and Lauren. He also became a father figure to myself and my younger brother Ryan. With our dad gone, he was the father figure we longed for.

Dave was an alcoholic who soon after marrying my mother, became abusive towards her. Despite this, we eventually moved into a lovely little bungalow in a nice area. Looking back, I think my mum only stayed with him in the hopes of a better life for us. That better life we had dreamed of, unfortunately wasn't the case — as I soon came to realise.

By age 11, it would be my responsibility to get the kids up in the morning and get them to preschool/school. I then had to go to the post office and cash my mum's cheque for her benefits and go to the shop to get what she needed. I would then make my way to school, always late and always getting in trouble. My only happy memories from living here was the safe refuge of my nan, I would call her from the phone box, well, I would do a reverse call, hang up and get her to call me back in the phone box — I'm sure she had that number saved due to me reverse calling her so much! I would explain what had happened at home and within half an hour, she was at the phone box picking me up to take me to her house. I loved my nan so much, she would look after me, show me love, and try to help me understand the ways of life. We lived in the bungalow for a couple of years before moving into a bigger house, apparently more room was needed with there being four of us siblings. This was when the issues started to appear more frequently. Dave continued to drink a lot, continued being abusive to my mother and he shouted and hit us if we misbehaved and we were scared! I mean truly scared because once you'd had one of his slaps, you didn't want another. He would threaten us with the belt he had too. Over time, more arguments occurred and then my mother fell into the trap of also drinking with him. They would often go to the pub together and leave me in charge of my siblings. They often went to the pub around dinner time and didn't return until the pub closed at midnight. When they returned it was always the same, arguing, smashing things up and me trying to keep the peace between them and protect the younger ones from seeing it when they were awoken by the noise. One evening I saw my mum have a full mental break-down, the TV went crashing on the floor from the wooden cabinet it was housed in, Dave was making it worse and my mum was slumped in the corner crying and rocking.

There was no consoling her, it was like a dog whimpering and cowering, his loud screams were deafening. I stood there shaking in fear and disbelief of what had happened. And even for a split second remember selfishly thinking how I'm meant to keep the kids occupied now — without a TV! I was used to this, but this was on a whole new scale. I saw my mum completely broken, like a little doll that you would wind up. The only thing she could do was rock... back and forth and cry. Just so much crying! I felt like she was always crying, she was always so sad. I had no idea what to do? I wasn't a psychologist or a doctor. I couldn't help her. She was so mentally poor anyway; I wasn't sure she could ever be fixed. As a child I saw her suffer from body dysmorphia, she would be in the bathroom and if we tried to speak to her through the door, she would scream at us and tell us to get away. As the oldest, I felt I was always responsible for checking in on her. She would often call me into the bath-room. She would ask if she had lots of dark hairs all over her face, I would say "no?" (she was fair-haired; she didn't even have dark vellus hair.) She had what seemed the normal number of tiny hairs on her face. She was so obsessed and would say I'm lying to her, or sometimes she would ask ten times if I would tell her the truth. I even remember her falling out with me, thinking I was lying to her. I was so sad and confused. Then she would turn around and stare into the one single mirror we were allowed to have in the house for the rest of the day or next few days. She hated mirrors, she hated pictures. You'd never find anything with her in it. She would spend her days obsessing over something that wasn't there, muttering how ugly she felt or was. I would do my best to reassure her, but I was a young (impressionable) girl, that didn't have the right things to say to her. I just felt so sad for her and for myself looking back, because the impact that had on me, even now, goes far deeper than I think she will ever understand. Over the years, I certainly felt like I picked up on these habits, the obsessing and the 'imposter syndrome'.

You are a result of your environment, if you know no better, you do no better. So even to this day, I still struggle massively with the way I look. I can't take compliments; I brush them off quickly and change the subject. I compare myself to others and I still sometimes cry in the mirror because I don't like what I see, but I'm working on that.

THE ESCAPE

I played the part of mum for quite some time, the only way I would be allowed out with any friends from school (the little I had) was if I babysat, then I would be allowed out. Oftentimes, this never happened, and I had to stay in. I could see my mum wasn't happy. She would often be online in my room, chatting to someone. Until one day my mum woke us up and told us to pack our bags! Scared and not knowing what was going on, I did as I was told and grabbed the bare minimum so we could move fast. It turned out she had met someone online and he was waiting around the corner to pick us up. I had never met this man in my life and as far as I knew at the time, neither had my mum! It turns out she had spoken to him online and they had devised a plan — he was taking us somewhere. He had even sent her a secret phone they could communicate on prior to this.

My mum must have finally realised that she needed to get away from Dave. All I can remember is being woken early and Dave was in the living room, drinking as usual. I remember having to run as fast as we could whilst he stumbled, shouted and started following us to the car in which this man was waiting. Ironically, his name was also Dave. We all jumped in the car as fast as we could, and we left. I remember it being a little car, red I think, we sat crammed in the back seat in silence. I looked up to see mum looking at this man in awe like he was her knight in shining armour. Whenever we spoke, we were told to keep quiet and I had to occupy David and Lauren whilst Ryan would be winding me up! I hated the entire drive and wanted to go home!

After an hour long, silent journey of confusion and fear, we arrived at what I guess was a meeting point where a lady took us to a women's refuge. It was cold, gloomy and the atmosphere was sad. The staff there tried to make it better but there were five of us living in one room. The timeframe we lived there for is vague, but the events weren't. It was a struggle, we were confined to a room, had a shared kitchen and bathroom and I could see my mum wasn't in a good place. One of my most vivid memories of that place was one night when I had woken and noticed my mum wasn't in the room. I ventured out of the room and found her in the kitchen. She was at the kitchen table alone, scissors in her hand and blood pouring from her inner wrist. She had sliced her wrist in an X shape. Whether she intended on attempting suicide I will never know. She quickly covered it up once she saw me crying and ordered me back to bed. The next morning it was like it had never happened and it was never spoken about again. Things always seemed to have that repeat cycle of something happening and then never being spoken about again.

After a while of being in the women's refuge, my mum got in contact with Dave (the one she met online). She announced we were moving to Ashton-under-Lyne to live with him. I protested that I did not want to go, but looking back, I think it was my mum's desperate and only attempt of fleeing the violence and sadness that we had all been going through. Of course, we couldn't stay at the refuge forever.

He picked us up and took us to a farmhouse that had a stable with horses attached to the side of it. He seemed quite well off in comparison to what we were used to. I later found out that he was helping my mum clear her debts. I had been set up on a folding camp bed in a room with one of my siblings. The room was dark; it wasn't decorated, and it most certainly wasn't welcoming. It was like we had been stuck under the stairs like Harry Potter! We weren't allowed to watch tv, he had one, but he would always be reading the newspaper and drinking his cups of black tea. Wanting silence.

Mum promised it wouldn't be forever, it was so we could have a better life. (I want to make it clear that in no way am I blaming my mum in this, I understand now at the age of 32 that she was doing what she thought was best. But uprooting your children and moving them to the middle of nowhere, with someone we did not know at all seemed so unfair). I missed my friends, I missed my little family, I missed school.

DEFIANT

For a whole year we stayed there, and I hated every second, this Dave was not much better than the last. He was controlling, miserable it was very much as if children should be seen, but not heard and he never spoke to us. In my eyes, I felt like we were a burden. The same thing happened again, I was left in charge of the other siblings and if I ever wanted to venture out, I had to do so by taking my younger sister Lauren in her pram. With no school there, I spent my days going into the local town. After a year of missing school, I asked my mum if I could move back to Blackpool, of course, she said no! I protested that I wanted to live with Dad (that was what I called Dave who was a father figure to me). After a year of being there and pushing my mum to her limits by shoplifting whilst I was out with my baby sister in town, she had enough and sent me back to live with Dave. It was during this time that one of the most pivotal times in my life began.

I moved back into the house we left, and he was suddenly overly nice. He made my bedroom look good; he still drank a lot but by now I was used to that. I was used to little food as any money he got went on drinking in the pub. From this age, it was when I truly began to realise that nobody was going to raise me except for myself. On the plus side though, I didn't have the responsibility of playing mum anymore, so I could go out and do anything I wanted. I eventually got myself a job working in a hotel. Back then you could get away with lying about your age, so I told them I was 16 (really I was only 14!) I worked hours on end just so I had some money, often, Dave would take this for drinking. I was working from 6am in the morning, getting the bus to work from Cleveleys to the North Promenade. I would sit on a bus for over an hour, sometimes having to get two buses which meant I had to get up even earlier. I was earning £2.75 per hour. Sometimes I would walk if I didn't have any money. I would work the breakfast shift, cleaning up, washing the pots and then I would move on and do the maid duties in over 60 rooms. With little staff, there was a lot to do and I wouldn't finish work until 9pm (if they needed staff to do the evening teatime wait service too) but for the first time in my life, I was earning money, my own money! My lovely nan was worried about me being so young and leaving work when it was dark, so she would collect me from work and take me home. I remember her being so proud of me and how hard I was working.

I know my nan was worried about the choices my mum had made and had asked her to come home, to no avail. I had no contact with her, I felt as if she were mad with me for betraying her and going back to live with Dave, but the truth was, I just wanted to be home, not away from everything I knew. Still living with Dave at the time, his drinking got worse and worse. He would often pass out on the sofa, soil himself, and so on. I just came in covered him up and went to bed. I remember one night, he had been drinking and I was in my bedroom, I was getting changed and out of the corner of my eye I saw a shadow and a small hole in the door. I had never noticed it until now. I was half undressed facing my mirrored wall he had made for me, with the door to the right of me. Only 14, I curiously went over to the door and investigated the hole. In complete shock, I saw something that I will never forget; Dave was spying through the door watching me get undressed! I felt sick, this was the person I called my dad, someone who had been around me since I was eight years old and he was watching me. As my eye met his, he quickly moved, and I jumped into bed. I was so confused, angry, upset and I didn't know what to think. *How long had he been watching me? Is that normal? Do dads do that? Is that why my real dad isn't around? Maybe I wasn't pretty enough for my real dad to spy on me, and that was why he left?* I cried into my pillow. I had nobody I could speak to about this without worrying them and I didn't know any different. I didn't know what dads were and weren't meant to do.

Trying to pretend it didn't happen as an instinct I had picked up, (or maybe just in denial and questioning whether it really happened) I went downstairs the next morning and he was still drinking, sitting in his dressing gown slumped in his chair. I sat down with my drink and pretended to watch TV; I think I was waiting for him to say something. The awkward silence felt like it went on for hours when in reality it was about 5 minutes. He sat there and to my disgust, he looked at me with his dirty, creepy eyes and opened his legs. Everything on show! I'm not quite sure what he expected me to do or say but my fight or flight mode kicked in and I sharply exited the room. I could hear him muttering and slurring "sorry" as I walked up the stairs. After that, I tried to pretend it didn't happen. After all, I didn't know what was right or wrong, I didn't have anywhere else to go. So I carried on as normal. Weeks later he told me we were moving to a new house, a brand-new house his sister owned, on a lovely estate. He exclaimed that he had seen it and had started decorating it for me. He also said that I could have the big room. I was so happy, I thought *maybe he's changing.*

THE NEXT STEP

Fast forward to the new house, I had a big double bed and he even rented me a sunbed. He stayed in the box room in a single bed and I thought maybe this was his way of apologising for what had happened. How wrong I was! I mean, why would a grown man want to sleep in a box room that barely fits a bed in it. I mean, I know he was too pissed half the time to even make it up there, but I did find it odd. But again, I told myself *it's because he wants me to have the best.*

My bedroom was lovely, it was all neutral colours, I made it my own and popped bits of pink everywhere — I was such a girly girl. When my friend would come over, I didn't care anymore about the state he was in because I had the coolest bedroom! Which is where we would stay most of the time anyway.

One day I was messing about with the pictures I had up, he had put a poster of some kind on the wall for me and I decided to see if it would look better somewhere else. It was a rainy day, I had nothing better to do, I had been on the sunbed and had a bath, then got changed into some clean clothes. I planned on just mucking about, chilling out and trying to keep busy, to pass time.

As I was cleaning my room, trying to change things up I started taking down a poster, this poster had been there before we moved in and I was sure Dave had put it up for decoration. I had never really noticed it as it was always hiding behind the open door. I noticed something strange, it was as if the paper had been ripped slightly and as I investigated it further, I pulled back the poster and noticed a hole! Fear and dread ran through every inch of my body. I peered through the hole and you could see right into the bathroom, specifically directly overlooking the bath! I went into the bathroom and noticed a really small hole I hadn't noticed before, I mean it was behind the bath, why would I notice it?

So, here I am wondering what is going on and I think back to the old house with the hole in the door. My so-called dad had again been spying on me, whilst I was on the sunbed from the bathroom or from my bedroom when I was in the bath. Sickened I ran around the corner to a friend I knew, and I told her in floods of tears. Even still, we didn't know what to do. I just knew that I needed to get out of that house.

With the best will in the world, I had no idea what I was going to do, I had nowhere else to go and I was too ashamed to tell anyone for fear of being bullied and not believed. I couldn't tell my mum at the time as we weren't in contact and I feared she may say something like "I told you what he was like!"

I ended up staying at a friend's house for a couple of days and then I found out that my mum was coming back to Blackpool. I was so relieved.

Once she was back, I moved in with her, but that didn't last long, by the age of 15 I was going out, getting into trouble, and again, my mum had enough. She kicked me out and refused to let me come home. The local authority office even tried to call her to liaise with her, but she wasn't taking me back. No way. I was homeless. One friend let me stay on her sofa for a couple of days but after that, I had to go and present myself to the local authority office, as being homeless. They housed me in a temporary B&B because there were no other options for me to go and stay anywhere, such as in care or supported accommodation, even with me being under the legal age of an adult. The B&B was on the other side of Blackpool, I had nowhere to go, I didn't know anyone and suddenly I felt all alone. I kept in contact with my nan, but I never wanted to worry her, so I didn't share the full story. I couldn't stay with her anyway and I would never have expected her to let me.

NEW BEGINNINGS

My friend had met a guy much older and he and some friends (I had just turned 16) went to a house party, everyone was taking drugs and drinking, and it was Christmas day. I didn't have any family to spend it with, so I thought I'd go and party instead. The party went on and one of the guys asked if anyone wanted to go to the shop, I said no, my friend insisted that I would go, whilst flirting with his friend. I felt pressured, so we set off to the shop. On the way there, he said "Come down this way, it's quicker", by this point I was paralytic, so I just stumbled after him. Suddenly, I remember him turning around and trying to kiss me, I pushed him away and said, "No, I don't want to." He continued to force himself upon me and I just froze, he pushed me to the ground, pulled up my dress and he raped me. I was so drunk at that moment that I had no idea what it truly felt like to even be able to describe it for you.

He got up and carried on walking to the shop and I just lay there hurting, wondering what on earth just happened! I was completely out of it. He came back and laughing said, "Come on, they'll think we've been up to no good." Even writing this makes my skin crawl. I had to go back into the house and pretend nothing happened. Shortly after I made a backdoor exit and did the long walk home in tears. The next few days passed, and I got a text from my so-called friend saying the local lads were all calling me a slag for sleeping with this guy down an alley. I was disgusted, I told her what happened, and she brushed it off and said something to the effect of, "Well that's not what everyone's saying." I never spoke about it again. I continued to be given abuse for what I had apparently done and eventually decided to stay away from that area. In all honesty, I didn't know at the time I had been raped. Although I didn't give my consent and told him no, I blamed myself for not fighting back harder and pushing him off me. We were never taught about consensual laws back then, it just happened, and I had to deal with it the best I could.

I would often have panic attacks, to the point where I couldn't breathe, and my chest felt so tight. At the time I was also experiencing a mix of emotions of self-blame as I mentioned before, but I was also angry. I was so f**king angry that he thought that was okay to do that to someone who was in no fit state to confirm a food order, let alone sexual intercourse.

This messed me up big time, I had no trust in men. By the age of 16 I had already been violated in ways nobody should have to. I would often compare my story though to other stories I had read, of rape or sexual abuse I had from Dave and I would justify this in my head like *Well it wasn't as bad as that so maybe I'm overreacting!* Even to this day, I still haven't shared this full story until now. I'm still finding ways of dealing with things.

During this time I met Daniel. I was only 16 when we met, and he was five years older than me. He was tall, dark and handsome, a bad boy and he seemed to be the one thing I needed. Someone that cared. However, he added a whole new chapter to my life that I wasn't prepared for. He was heavily into drinking and recreational drugs, something I was easily led into. It went from just doing it at the weekend to becoming a daily thing where the binge sessions would last up to five days with no sleep and constant drugtaking. After only being together for three months, he was sent to jail and I waited around 4 months for him to get out. I was an impressionable 16-year-old back then and he was the only person I felt that got me. Daniel, unfortunately, wasn't very well mentally, he suffered from schizophrenia and psychosis. He was on medication but all the recreational drugs he took cancelled out the positive impact that his medications were meant to have on him. He had a very difficult upbringing involving violence and drugs. I was becoming someone I didn't want to be, but I was stuck between that and being in love with him. And so it continued.

MOVING ON AND MOVING IN

After two years I eventually got the council flat I wanted! I moved in there with nothing, it was cold with tile floors. There were storage heaters that would take three days to come on. By now I was living closer to my nan and she was helping me buy little bits of furniture from a second-hand shop. I had a bed, a sofa, and just the kitchen essentials. She helped me the best she could, but she was living on a pension and didn't have much money for herself let alone me. I decided to enrol in college and do a level 3 Travel & Tourism course. Finally, I was working towards something. I often missed my course because I was too busy with my boyfriend or going out but eventually did pass my course at 19. Shortly after that, during a five-day drug-fuelled binge, I started being sick, thinking nothing of it except for the fact it was probably because I hadn't slept and was still taking numerous drugs. I don't say this because it's something I'm proud of by any means at all, but I say this so as the reader you can truly see the level of despair that it got to. I had completely lost myself. That working, enthusiastic girl with a willingness to make a change in life. She had gone.

Eventually, I went home and slept it off.

The next day, I said to Daniel, I can't keep doing this, it's making me unwell and I don't want this for myself. As usual it ended up in a big argument and we split up. You must remember that I had been with this guy for three years at this point. I thought he was the love of my life and I couldn't understand why he would want to keep doing the same things. Five years older than me, surely, he was bored with it. I tried to get him into college, into jobs, but nothing ever worked. He had his life plan, and I wasn't a part of it unless I wanted to keep doing the same things. I would sometimes stay at his house, his mum, who hated me, always assumed I was the bad one that was getting him into all sorts when it was the complete opposite way around. I wanted to help her son, I loved her son and I wanted to see him come out of the other side of this with me. After only being together for three months, he was sent to jail and I waited around 4 months for him to get out. I was an impressionable 16-year-old back then and he was the only person I felt that got me. Daniel, unfortunately, wasn't very well mentally, he suffered from schizophrenia and psychosis. He was on medication but all the recreational drugs he took cancelled out the positive impact that his medications were meant to have on him. He had a very difficult upbringing involving violence and drugs. His mum had mollycoddled him and reinforced how poorly he was, looking back it was like Munchausen syndrome. I don't think it was because she didn't care about him, but perhaps the opposite. She didn't want him near me. I never understood why she didn't like me, but I don't think she was as stable as she liked to make out. He essentially knew no better after the life he'd had. Being the empath I am, loving him and wanting him to change, we decided he should live with me, by this stage I had I turned 18 and I had my council flat finally. I would become his caregiver. At first, it worked, but his medication would make him sleepy, snappy and then he would refuse to take it. I would try to speak to his mental health worker to find ways we could help him, to no avail. He would disappear for days on end with no contact and then one day I said I wasn't doing it anymore. I was sick of him being at parties with other girls and hearing all sorts of stories of what he had been up to, I decided to do something that I will forever regret. I knew it was over for good, he didn't care about me, he was more interested in partying and being out.

I made a call to my nan and I told her that I loved her, I then took 38 paracetamols with vodka. The next thing I remember is being in the ambulance with my nan. My poor beautiful nan must have known something was wrong and had come to check on me. She had a key, let herself in, and found me on the floor crying with packets of tablets everywhere. I was taken to the hospital and was telling the nurses I didn't want to be alive anymore if I couldn't be with the person that I felt I loved the most. I truly felt like I had nothing to live for. At the hospital, I was allowed to make a call, I called Daniel and asked him to come and see me in hospital (despite my nan's pleas not to!) and explained what I had done, unsurprisingly he was too busy at a party and didn't want to see me. I was devastated that for three years I had confided in this man; I had told him my life story and everything that I had been through.

Shortly after, my mum who was now back in Blackpool came to the hospital, she took my phone and told me I was going to stay with my nan for a few days so she could look after me. I remember sitting in her little car looking out of the window, I was staring into my own little world, watching as the world went by as normal. I quickly took off my belt as she was driving, opened the door and tried to jump out. It was so selfish and looking back as a mother myself now, I can't even comprehend how she must have felt but it was so real. I didn't want to be here anymore. My mum's reflexes must have been insanely fast because the speed I did that was with intention, but her intention must have been just as strong too.

TIME WITH NANNY BEAR

A couple of days later I was at my nan's house and she offered me a fried egg sandwich, I said "No thanks nan, I've gone off egg lately." She looked at me with concern and asked whether I thought I could be pregnant, I smirked it off and said, "No way!" She suggested we get a test just to be sure and nipped to my Aunty Bev's house where I did the test. I walked into the room and burst into tears. I was pregnant with my first child! I was 19, I had no idea how to raise a child. I was still learning how to raise myself! I spoke with Daniel and we discussed the fact that we both didn't have a Dad growing up, but we wanted to change and make this work even though I lived in an unfurnished council house and was only getting about £50 a week to live off.

At this point I felt so guilty, the stupid things I had done, attempting suicide, and the drugs I had been taking. I needed to get on the straight and narrow. I decided to keep the baby and fortunately, the baby was blessed to be perfectly healthy.

It wasn't long before Daniel was up to his old tricks, but this time I wasn't standing for it. I decided that I would do it alone if I had to and I did. I went through the pregnancy on and off with him, trying to make him understand that this baby needed a father, but nothing seemed to work. He was so set in his ways.

Our child was born a healthy 7lb 3oz boy. He was beautiful, he took my breath away from the moment I met him. I settled into being a new mum and tried so hard to do as much as I could to be the best possible parent, but things were still so unresolved in my mind. I found myself back in with the wrong crowd doing all the wrong things. It took me the first six months of his life and missing out on what is the most special time for a parent, to realise that I needed to stop. I was a mess. I was still there but I was never present with him and still to this day it haunts me. If I could go back and redo those months again, I would in a heartbeat.

Just as I was getting myself back on track, Daniel appeared, but this time he wasn't playing, he wanted contact with his son. I had tried to get access through the courts for him, but he would never show. I put my foot down and made a choice to keep my son safe and away from anything he was up to. I have still to this day, never blamed him, and to this day he hasn't had any contact with him directly, but I know that it's something he deeply regrets now. We have had contact over the years, and he has expressed how sorry he is for the choices he made, but he could still never be the true role model I need for my son. Not unless he was completely clean from drugs and in control of his mental health. We often talk, he messages me once a year or so, sometimes more frequently. There's no bad blood with us, I chose to forgive him a long time ago. He was never a bad person; he just made bad choices. I still now let him see pictures of Rico and we discuss meeting up one day. Unfortunately, the time still isn't right for him as he still makes the same choices he did before. I pray one day, for my Rico's sake, that he gets the closure he needs by being able to meet his biological dad. My intention was never to keep him from him, but from his choices and actions. I never thought he would harm Rico, but I just couldn't trust that he would be in the right frame of mind to be a dad. I still don't think he will ever understand the true extent of what he put us through though, despite his apologies.

It was around 2am and I was getting prank calls. I answered one and it was Daniel at a party and had said, "If I can't have you and my son, then nobody will!" He told me in detail how he was going to come to our home with a machete and kill us both, "Chop us both up" or me in front of our son and let Rico grow up witnessing the fact his dad killed his mum. After years of hearing things like this you become numb to it.

49

I was scared but I didn't think he would actually do it! The next thing I know, there's banging at the door. I didn't answer in fear of it being him but instead, it was the police. To this day I will never fully know how they found out, but they came in, told me to grab my son and anything I needed quickly, and get in their car. This was on Christmas Eve, it was about to be my son's first Christmas, he was just 9 months old. I was told nothing; it was pitch black and I was taken to a safe house in the middle of nowhere where we stayed for six months. They took my phone, I wasn't allowed contact with anyone. After around three weeks I was allowed to call my nan and let her know what had gone on. She had been worried sick. I couldn't tell her where I was or what had happened in too much detail. I just told her that I loved her.

Around a month later the police apprehended Daniel after he went on the run. They told me they had received a call from someone who was concerned for us. With him already being very well known by the police for being dangerous, they had to act fast. I was advised to move out of Blackpool as soon as I could. At the time I couldn't, I had no money, so I had to stay in a women's refuge until I had saved enough. Over time I was slowly allowed out but could only meet people in town centres and couldn't tell anyone where I was living, not even those I trusted, such as my nan.

THE NEXT HORIZON

I had started chatting to a new guy, things were good, and I had met up with him a few times. He invited me to Bolton where I met a friend of his we will call her Sarah. One night, Sarah was having a party and said she had her daughter and to bring my son so we could all have a few drinks. I went there with the guy I had been talking to and she seemed nice. After a few drinks I confided in her about what had happened, and she told me that I could come and stay with her. There was no reason not to, it was a fresh start. I needed to get out of Blackpool, and she was offering to let me and my son stay as long as we needed. I told my nan, who of course worried and told my mum, who at the time didn't really seem that interested, which pushed me even further to go. I secretly returned to Blackpool and a friend of mine helped me move my things to Bolton once I had found somewhere. Things fizzled out with the guy I was seeing from Bolton, but the friendship with Sarah grew stronger. Over time, I started to notice she would like to have parties a lot. I couldn't say much as she was letting me live there rent-free, I just had to help around the house and maybe watch her child from time to time.

The parties got more regular and one night after the kids were in bed asleep, I remember walking into the kitchen and seeing them with a pipe and white stuff. After questioning what it was (I knew what cocaine was but didn't know what they were doing with the pipe). They all laughed, and Sarah told me to sit down and she would make me a drink. It was a dark-coloured drink and when I asked what it was, she just replied "Just drink it!" Feeling embarrassed from them laughing at me, I knocked back the drink. Shortly after I remember feeling slow and I can't remember anything from that moment until I woke up to Sarah shouting at me, "Get up and sort your kid out, you've not moved off the sofa for two fucking days, it's not my responsibility to look after your kid!" I remember my son in the travel cot in the front room crying. Confused and dumbfounded I didn't believe I had been out of it for two days! Sure as anything, I checked my phone, and it was 1:40pm on a Sunday. The party was Friday night. What the hell had I been given? I felt overwhelmed with guilt, sadness and I was scared! My only thought now was that it must have been spiked with something. I still had nowhere to go, but I was going to the local council daily pushing for help to find a place to stay. Eventually, I was accepted for help with finding a house and I found one locally that Sarah had suggested. The house was awful, but I needed to get out. I needed to get out of that environment.

After moving into this house, I can only describe it as a heavily Indian/Pakistani area. I must have been one of the only Caucasian women there. I had no issues with this, not until I started getting guys knocking at the door. The front door was glass and directly off the living room, so I had no way of hiding, except if I stayed upstairs which is what I usually did.

After a while of being there I got speaking to a girl we will call Jen, she and her sister lived on the same street with their parents, but I hadn't noticed as I barely left the house. One day Jen sparked up a conversation with me and suggested she come round to help me decorate and get settled in. I kindly took her up on the offer and we became (what I thought, were friends) She introduced me to her sister and her sister would sometimes babysit so I could go to Blackpool and see friends, or my friends could come to me and we could have a night out.

Not too long after, Sarah heard of my friendship and after confiding in Jen, she had told her all my secrets and my reasons for not speaking to her anymore, another betrayal. Sarah decided to make my life hell. She would spread rumours around about me that I was sleeping with the lads on the street and because I was new to the area, the lads outside of the area sometimes ventured down to my street to see the new girl and try their luck. Of course, this didn't appeal to Sarah and she continued to speak to other girls and turn them against me. Even going as far as telling her group of girl and guy friends that I had an STI (sexually transmitted disease) which wasn't the case! I was back to feeling lonely, but at least I had my son.

ROSE-TINTED GLASSES

After a while of being in Bolton and staying in, I tried Facebook to make new friends. I received a friend request from someone called Alex. We got chatting and he sounded like a good guy! By this point, I had no friends, no babysitters, nothing so he suggested coming round once my son was in bed so we could have a date night, watch a film and have some food. Ever the gent he turned up and wowed me with his words, he was charming and didn't live far from me. Our relationship progressed and we soon became boyfriend and girlfriend. I thought I had finally found my happy ending. I told him I had trouble trusting people and when he asked why I moved to Bolton, I told him the truth about my past. He knew of Sarah and had warned me about her saying I got in with the wrong crowd. Time went on and all alone, I came to rely on him. I met his family and his mum (God rest her soul) and finally felt like a had a little family.

However, it wasn't the fairy tale I had hoped for. I'd receive messages from girls telling me he had been with them, which he denied, and told me it was because "people were jealous", but this was happening more frequently and then he started to lose his temper. I started to become scared of him but had fallen into yet another trap of wearing my heart on my sleeve and thinking that I loved the guy! I got myself a job working in sales and made a friend through work, the job gave me some independence and allowed me to try and settle into my new life. Alex didn't like the job; didn't like I had made friends and would often make comments about my new friend. In reality he was just trying to isolate me.

Eventually, after just three months out of nowhere, he broke up with me, I was devastated and felt alone. I spent the days in bed with my son, isolated to the house due to people being nasty outside it, and then suddenly felt a feeling I remembered very well. I was pregnant again! I had been on the contraceptive pill so was confused about how this had happened. When I called, he wouldn't answer, so I had to text him the news and he even had the nerve to ask me if it was his! We had only known each other for three months; my head was well and truly gone.

By this stage I had a better relationship with my mum and had friends back home I could speak to. Although she only visited me once in the entire time I lived in Bolton, I felt like the move had strengthened our relationship through distance. My friends and family advised me that having a baby with this guy was the wrong thing to do.

I rang him and asked if we could meet. He came around and ended up getting upset to the point of tears, begging me to keep the baby. Yet another guy without a father figure in his life, he decided we should keep the baby and try and make things work. At first I said no. We couldn't go a day without arguing. What kind of life was that going to be for our unborn child and my son?

After a long discussion and lots of promises, we tried again. Unfortunately, things never got better only worse. I would find blatant messages in his phone from girls he had been meeting whilst I'd be at home carrying his child. I was so vulnerable by this stage and so isolated that he could easily talk me round and after half an hour, it was like it had never happened. One of the girl's names I remember was Gemma, I found messages, explicit ones, ones with plans and about their night. He didn't live with me, so I had no idea what he was up to. I'll get back to Gemma soon.

As time passed, things got heavy, he would start with screaming in my face, apologise, then we would make up. Then it started with pushing and shoving and more increasingly it became physical acts of punishment if I didn't do as I was told or dared question what he had been up to. I remember a day where my friend from work came around, we had been having movie day with sweets with my son and Alex turned up, he wasn't happy, but she was there. He wanted to speak to me in the kitchen on my own. I asked her to take my son upstairs just in case anything untoward happened, she did and out of nowhere he gripped me by the throat, slammed my back against the kitchen worktop and started strangling me. I remember the feeling so perfectly, whether this was the moment I was going to die. I couldn't catch my breath, he just continued to squeeze and squeeze until I had no breath left in me and felt like I was going to pass out. My friend came flying downstairs screaming at him to get off me. He pushed her out of the way, resulting in back-handing her (leaving her with a bruise to the eye). He then continued to grab me, push me hard onto the floor and kick me in the stomach. Crying my eyes out I was worried sick for the safety of not only my friend but my baby as I had already landed on my stomach. At this stage I was very heavily pregnant so worried there was a chance I would lose the baby.

Events like this weren't uncommon, the odd slap, the back-hander, twisting my arm, grabbing my hair, and pulling me off the sofa or bed. Anything he could do to remain in control and feel powerful. On this occasion when my friend was there the reasoning behind why he flipped out, was because he did not like the thought that I had been confiding in her about our problems. Unfortunately, shortly after this event I lost my only friend, she couldn't be around somebody who was emotionally draining her, by going back to a man who continuously bullied her, especially whilst carrying a baby. At the time I was so angry that she could just abandon me. Now I understand the negative impact this must have had on her, watching someone she cared about promising to leave, and not put up with it, but always going back. I was stuck in a trap and he was isolating me from anyone that told me any different from what he told me.

This cycle went on and on, with the abuse getting worse. While I was pregnant, the landlord of the house I was in wanted to sell and needed me out. He gave me two weeks' notice to find somewhere else. Luckily for me, my boss at the time had a house he was renting out that he let me move into without having to put a bond down. But he had tenants in it at the time, so I had to go to Bolton Council and show them my eviction notice. I was moved to the opposite side of Bolton from Alex in sheltered accommodation, in a rough area and all alone. It was awful, I still remember the stench of wee that came from the flat.

I stayed there for about five months and then moved into the newer house my boss owned. Alex moved in and the violence continued. One day I started bleeding, so I went to the hospital. The doctors examined me, the same as they did at the beginning for all health checks. This time they found out the bleeding was coming from something unrelated to violence. It was related to me having an STI! So, during my relationship with Alex, I of course hadn't been near anyone else, the only answer to this question was that he had, and he had passed this on to me. I spent the whole day in hospital albeit he was there with me after he finished work denying it. I was so drained I had no fight left in me. My son was at home and I remember asking Alex if he could please go home and take over whilst they kept me in hospital. For hours they couldn't find the baby's heartbeat, I was worried sick. He proclaimed he couldn't as he had to work. Thinking nothing of it, he left. I was later informed by someone I knew that he was seen getting picked up from the hospital by Gemma! The girl that he had slept with behind my back whilst carrying his child and assumingly received the STI from.

I'm lying on the hospital bed crying; they still couldn't find the heartbeat and I had to wait hours for them to scan me. Thank the lord that they eventually did, and my baby was doing okay. During that scan that he didn't bother sticking around for because he was on a date with Gemma, he missed the opportunity to find out that we were going to be having a girl.

TRYING TO LEAVE

O ur beautiful baby girl was born in 2011 on my birthday, the 26th of November. She weighed a tiny 6lb 7oz. I was so in love with her! Just as I was with her brother.

Again, after the birth of our daughter, we tried to make it work. Yes, stupid I know, but in my distorted mind that was riddled with anxiety, loneliness, and depression, I needed someone there. I figured the baby might be the glue that holds us together to make him change. We moved into a new house and I finally started to feel myself getting back on track. I wanted to enrol in college in Bury, it was about an hour away on the bus from where I lived, two bus journeys, and my son was at nursery. I asked him if he could help me whilst I went to college to study criminology and he agreed. I enrolled and felt a sense of pride that things were looking up, until one day he decided that he didn't want to help anymore, so I had to quit.

By this stage it had been almost two years of the same cycle of abuse and isolation. I decided to go back to Blackpool and visit my nan and my mum. They were desperate to get me back there, offering to help me find a house but I was so scared, it took me months before I finally decided I needed to go home. I was no longer scared of Daniel after everything I had been through with Alex.

When I went down to see them, I pretended I was visiting family, but really, I was checking out houses so I could escape. I remember asking Alex to move to Blackpool with me before this, he had said "No way, never" he also threatened me. "If I ever tried to leave and take his kids away, he would kill me."

I had gone from one mentally abusive relationship and straight into another. My only plan was to wait for him to leave (he had gone back to his mum's at this point due to the arguments being so bad again) and then pack my things. I had to pack what I could, and I arranged to be picked up in the middle of the night to flee the violence. My mum had said she would pay for the bond and rent upfront for the house we eventually found. She and my nan just wanted us all back and safe.

HOME TIME

I eventually got back to Blackpool and started trying to rebuild my life all over again with two children on my own. It was difficult, but this was nothing in comparison to the lifestyle I had been living before. I decided at that moment that things needed to change, and I had to stop making decisions that were detrimental to not only my health but also to my children. One of the main things I remember however, was moving back to Blackpool and having no money. I was shopping with my nan, and I went to the self-checkout and remember looking at the total and realising I didn't have enough, so I pretended to scan some baby milk and nappies. Of course, I got caught, my poor nan was mortified, and we were taken out the back. They didn't care when I explained in floods of tears, that it was because I was short on money, I just needed food. I hadn't bought or stolen anything for myself, it was for the kids, but the security staff were having none of it! They made me feel so low! My nan even offered to pay, and they declined, they insisted on calling the police. I got away with a warning and was banned from the shop. I was so embarrassed and mortified for my nan who had no idea what had been going on. I didn't want to ask her for money as I already owed her some. The worst part was having to declare it for a job I wanted later at a children's home. Luckily, the owner of the home I wanted to work at completely understood as I sat there bright red and fighting back the tears, that's how poor I was! I had to steal to feed my children. It was such a low point in life but if it meant my children were fed, I would have done it again in all honesty. Just not with my nan there!

Once I was back home, things were good and bad with my mum. She had come such a long way with her issues she had from younger years and she had my gorgeous baby sister Lucy. Lucy had Down's syndrome, so she was her full-time caregiver. The sweetest little ray of sunshine you could ever meet. The relationship between my mum and I was always a little all over the place. We never spoke and even now, unfortunately to this day, things have never been solid with us for long. However, I had to tell her at one point what had happened with Dave as I had heard that he was wanting contact with my siblings now they were older. She cried, apologised, protested we go to the police, but I just wanted to move on from it. I reassured her it wasn't her fault, but I had to let her know as he now wanted contact with David and Lauren, and if he could do that to me, what was to say he wouldn't do it to her? I had to protect my sister. Unfortunately, to this day the relationship between me and my mum still isn't there. I've never quite been sure why and it hurts to know you have a mother, who you have passed in the street and just ignored you. I often feel sad and upset that not only did my dad not want me, but neither did my mum. I think that's why I cling to my nan so much; she has always been the only one that's never given up on me.

I decided to enrol in university and I studied health and social care at a foundation degree level. I finally started to feel like I had some purpose in life. Confidence was still at an all-time low but as the days went on, I was rebuilding my life so that I could make a better future for my children. Fast forward to around a year later, Alex was still harassing me, he would constantly call, and text and I had explained to him that I had no problem with him seeing the children if it was to see the children and not to see me. Alex wouldn't make the journey to Blackpool to see the children so the only way that the children could have any contact with Alex would be if I got the train to drop them off and the train to collect them, with no maintenance being paid from him. I was struggling. Eventually I put my foot down and explained to him that if he wanted to see the children he would need to come and meet me halfway or do one of the journeys. Eventually, he agreed that he would come and either collect the children or drop them off. We had agreed to meet at a shop which wasn't too far from where we were now living. I didn't want him knowing where we lived for our safety, but he would continuously push to try and find our address. On one of the occasions, he played a game with our son (I say our because my son decided from a young age that he wanted to call him Daddy. I of course said no, but Alex insisted that it was only right, and he couldn't have one child grow up calling him Daddy and not the other). During this game he asked our son, if he could show Daddy the way home and he would give him some money. Sure enough our son showed him exactly where we lived. My son didn't know any better due to being so young. From then on, the bullying ways and the terrorising started again. He would be outside the house, he would call and say he was coming unannounced and it got too much, I started to get worried again and had to log it with the police. The final and possibly one of the most heart-breaking moments of the whole situation was when he turned up at the house. He barged in, I had our daughter who was just one in my arms, he pushed me back and I landed with my back smashing the stairs, I got up and told him to get out. He was accusing me of seeing other guys, at this stage I was angry and told him that even if I was, it was none of his business. As I fell back, my phone fell out of my pocket, he quickly grabbed it and saw a notification from a male friend. He went crazy! Still holding our daughter, he kept pushing me and pushing me, I fell back again on the stairs and he threw punches and kicks at me as I lay there trying to protect our daughter. My son came running into the hall crying and screaming, "Daddy get off Mummy, you're hurting her!" He was so upset it still breaks my heart to this day remembering it. He pushed him and told him to get out and go into the front room, but he continued to stand there begging for Daddy to leave Mummy alone. For a split second he stopped, looked at me and I just saw this anger in his face, he grabbed my fingers and twisted them back trying to snap them, he then grabbed me by my hair, smacked my head off the step, pulled me towards him and attempted to bite my off my ear. As soon as I got a split second, I grabbed the children and ran out of the house screaming. Luckily, the neighbours across the road saw me hysterically crying and bleeding and called the police. During the whole cycle of violence I never followed through with reports with the police, I was too scared. He had never done it in front of the kids before this, but he told me they wouldn't believe me anyway. He threatened to punch himself to make it look like I did it! It was crazy. But that was it, it was the first and final time I was going to let my kids witness the things I had seen growing up.

Within 30 seconds he was gone, with my phone in hand. He went on the run for over a month before the police finally found him. As soon as he was caught, he was remanded to Preston Prison for 30 days. When it came to court, he was issued a £40 fine! The laws around domestic violence are now much stronger but I genuinely believe that I was failed by the justice system. They had pictures of my injuries but because he had stolen my phone, I had no evidence of the threats and harassment, so, it was my word against his. He had a solicitor that he paid for and I had a legal aid one. His solicitor turned the whole thing around on me during the court case. It was torturous, I was made to feel like I was the one to blame, as I stood in the dock, in floods of tears trying to catch my breath, only to be tormented that "Only the guilty cry when they realise the truth is prevailing!" that I was the one that inflicted the pain on him, like I deserved what had happened to me! I'll never forget that day, walking out of the court on my own after being annihilated by a solicitor. I felt so small, so invisible, and worst of all, I felt like I had let my children down, again. The justice system let me and my children down that day and it made me think *No wonder people don't report this kind of thing!*

CHRISTMAS 2016

I remember the Christmas of 2016, I was poor, and I mean counting pennies for milk and raiding the back of the sofa for pennies poor. I was in such a bad place and I struggled heavily with social anxiety and depression. I hated the way I looked and in my head I would beat myself up about the life I was giving my kids, wondering if I was good enough for them. I swear by the holy universe that if it weren't for my two beautiful children I wouldn't be here today writing this book. I looked at them with their big, beautiful blue eyes, with eyelashes to die for, their gorgeous blonde hair and I looked at how much they adored me. To them, it didn't matter that they didn't have brand new toys, new clothes. I was their superstar, I was amazing. All they wanted was to be loved. I couldn't do that to them, I couldn't let them grow up without proving to them that one day, Mummy was going to make it, so we never went without. That Christmas of 2016, I sat there as they opened their Pound Shop presents that I had got with a payday loan of £100 that I knew I wouldn't be able to pay back and my heart broke for them. I had to make something of myself and prove everyone wrong. Prove to all those that had called me thick, stupid, never going anywhere in life that I was going somewhere. I was never going to feel this feeling of guilt or failure again.

After surviving two heavily abusive relationships I put all my energy into trying to learn how to live for myself. I went to university and graduated with my foundation degree; I then completed my honours degree and finally my PGCE which enabled me to teach students over the age of 16. My time at university was so much fun, my best friend Connie of (now) 17 years was there with me. We always got told off for talking too much! We laughed, we cried, we messed about. I felt like I was becoming me again thanks to the help of having such a beautiful, loyal best friend to help me through the hard times, some of which she could relate to unfortunately. Still to this day she remains my closest friend and confidante. My love for her will always be there. No matter how busy life gets, we always pick up where we left off, like we had never been apart. Just one more thing to love her for.

During university I had several jobs, I worked late hours, night shifts, and worked in mental health and with young children. I loved it, but I always had that hunger for more.

After some time passed, I began to let Alex back into the children's lives and they started visiting him fortnightly. He now had a new girlfriend, and he was focused on her so he would leave me to my own devices. I wouldn't receive any help from him maintenance wise, but I was grateful, and still am that he continued to raise my son as his own; despite everything we had been through. I explained that he needed to speak to our son about what had happened. I didn't want him to grow up thinking that it's okay to do that kind of thing, I didn't want it to become a vicious cycle thinking it's okay to hurt women or anyone for that matter. I needn't have worried, he is growing up to be the most loving, loyal, and kind-hearted boy I know. Alex and I haven't always seen eye to eye, but as I mentioned, I do have respect for the fact that for the last 11 years, he's raised my son as his own.

With things on amicable grounds with Alex and never hearing from Daniel again by this point, I had to focus on getting my life in order. I passed my theory test and bought my first car, I went on my first girls' trip and even paid for the children's first trip abroad. Life was finally looking up, but it was killing me. I was still beating myself up that I wasn't doing good enough. I needed more. I owed it to myself and to my kids to show them that their mum wasn't going to be a victim, but a badass survivor!

I set up my own little side business and started making money. I didn't have a clue about business, I didn't know the ins and outs of how to run one, I just did a training course and started doing some teeth whitening from home. I invested in a machine and a beauty bed with my student finance and fortunately for me, the business took off. It was booming, I had at least ten clients a day. I started thinking more strategically, how could I make this even better? So, any profit I made, I saved and I invested in another machine and bought another beauty bed. Now I was making twice as much in the same amount of time. I did this for around a year whilst working at a college teaching 16-year-olds, studying at a postgraduate degree level, and raising two children, I was exhausted! But I didn't care that fire in my belly was pushing me harder and harder every day. I'm not going to say it was easy, I had to work all the hours under the sun, sometimes until 11pm doing treatments. Then waking up at 5am to get the kids to school and nursery to get to the college.

One day, towards the end of my time working in the college, I was asked if I was going to apply to be a teacher full time by a fellow student on my course. I hesitated, because by now, I had been in touch with a girl about doing some skincare courses, and this idea of working for myself appealed to me. But again, I had no idea what to do in business, I had no idea where it would even lead. So, I decided I'm not going to work for someone else's dream, I'm going to work for my own! It was a huge risk; it was outside my comfort zone and I had no idea whether or not it would work.

Fuck what anyone thought. I was going to prove everyone was wrong about me. I was going to prove to my mum that I wasn't going to be the single mum with a kid in a council flat, that she told my brother and sister not to turn out like! My life was about to step up massively. I had no idea or plan how, but I was going to make it happen.

I missed nights out with my friends, I had to cut people off that weren't going on the same journey as me. I had to find a way to change and grow. I lost friends I thought had my back from day one, that's life it happens. Sometimes you just outgrow people, and you need to focus more on yourself. Whether that's selfish or not, I had to do it to ensure I made up for the things that had happened and make the life I was desperate for. It was never about being rich. I was already rich in love, health, safety, and my children (and of course my beautiful nan). It was about moving things out of my way that no longer served me well. Cutting any drama, cutting any negativity, and moving into the path I needed to be on.

I needed to not only change my life but my mindset too, I had to stop feeling like the world was out to get me and start seeing the positives. I have always been spiritual, always believed in a hierarchy and the Law of Attraction, so, I started implementing this into my life. I'm a strong believer that what you give, you get, what you think about you will become and whether you think you can or think you can't — you're right!

GAME CHANGER LEVEL

I signed up with a company and started doing training courses. I added these and started expanding the treatments I offered. I had seen a girl online, she looked like she was living the dream, kitted out in the nicest clothes, going on regular holidays, offering highly discounted courses. I decided to go for it. This girl seemed like she was successful!

Arriving early with my models and not knowing much different, the shop I went to do these courses seemed a lot different in real life to what she was portraying online. The girl I had seen online was there and I was in awe of her. She seemed to have it all, a Rolex, a new GLA Mercedes and she was telling me how Mercedes was hounding her offering their newest cars for free! I thought *Wow! This is what I want!*

She looked like she was living the dream, so how was her amazing, busy, sold out training courses doing so well, when all she had was a little rundown shop that she had nick-named the little shop of dreams?! It was absolutely awful, unsanitary and so poorly run. I was there, I had paid, I needed to get these courses done so that I had more strings to my bow. I had paid for five courses upfront and was going to make them work. Well, what a disaster that was! To be quite honest, I'm not even going to give her the airtime by naming her, she doesn't deserve it. Let's just say I had to make do with what I was given at the time, and to be honest, I didn't have much to compare it to. I just know I felt like I was walking away with little knowledge and help with what I had paid for. However, she was very persuasive, she told me all these people she had helped who were making thousands and how she had changed their life. I left and went away and worked hard to research more to try and make the money I had spent, into more money and better skills. I decided that I needed to look for somewhere that I could rent so that I would look more professional. I went in search of a property and I found one. I remember telling her about it, it was huge and needed a lot of work done. There were holes in the walls, flooring needing replacing, it was derelict. Completely rundown and it was going to be a huge challenge! I signed a piece of paper after speaking to the landlord and that was it! I had a huge building and I had to try to make this work. I would work, save, and then buy something new. For the first year, I was confined to one room that my brother and I had painted (awfully by the way) carrying out treatments. One day I got a message from this girl asking why I don't start offering training for the courses I did. By now I had researched a lot, I had my teaching experience and she offered to come and teach other courses that I couldn't teach. She would provide the paperwork and certificates, all I needed to do was advertise the training and she would come and do it. It seemed like the perfect plan to get myself off the ground. Her idea was, that she had trained someone else locally in the beauty side and that I should get her in to do that side. We could join up and make a bigger business. I felt like it was going to be the best idea ever!

Lucky for me, I had just gotten into a relationship with James at the time. He was gorgeous, kind-hearted and he wanted to help me succeed. I felt like the luckiest girl in the world! He helped me renovate the place, just paying for materials and in return whenever I would start to make some money, I would treat him. He was incredible and finally, I had found someone that was treating me like a queen!

So, I had a girl we will call Amy in one room doing her beauty and I was in another doing my skincare and I had James helping me make the place look better. After a while I started to notice cracks in things, the paperwork this girl was sending out for me to teach students was abysmal, I would be teaching facials and it would have content in it about spray tans. She would turn up late to any training I had booked for her, looking like she had been out partying the night before, arriving in dirty scrubs and would sit on her phone, not even acknowledging the students when she finally arrived. After a word with her and some complaints from students, I was promised that things would improve. I was paying her most of the course cost to teach, money for the paperwork, money for the certificates to be sent out that would often arrive with the wrong names and most of the time the things I needed didn't even arrive. I was also paying her academy a licence fee of £50 a month on top of this. I was barely making any money. After speaking with the tutor with all the knowledge and money, she told me I was ready to go to the next level. This was her way to defer the situation, by blaming the staff in the office for any wrongdoings. She had me completely brainwashed!

This time she was offering to come and teach injectable fillers and anti-wrinkle injections. She told me this was where the money was at and I could charge £1500 and get four girls at a time on the courses. In return she would give me a small cut. And so, we did. The offer flew out, I had 24 girls booked on this double training course for her to come and teach and I was fully booked for the whole year! I would get a small cut (or offers on more training courses) and she would get the main bulk. I was still paying for certificates and coursework fees that flew up in price as well as my monthly licence fee. In all honesty, I wasn't making much money at all. Any bookings that were made she would have the money transferred from my account to hers, so all bookings went through my business and she got paid.

The first training date we had (one every month was being held with at least 3 or 4 girls on each date) was in January. She had so many girls booked in altogether that she had been paid for. Anyway, on the first date, as usual, she arrived late looking the same, like she had been out partying all night, didn't even speak to the students and went and slumped herself on the sofa. I had to do all the introductions and welcome and she would just show them how to inject, leave them to it, and leave. Each student had models, I was told that they all needed eight models; five filler models at £89 and three anti-wrinkle models at £100, she was being handed cash of around £745 per training student. All these models were crammed into two days her PPE was not in place, no prescriptions for models being carried out (that I now know, both are paramount) and it was just a disaster. She was there for the money and nothing else. I could sense the students weren't happy and it was raising anxiety in me that I thought I had under control. I needed to do something about this as she had 24 girls booked in for the rest of the year.

She had promised me that during this time, for a discounted rate of £1000 she would teach me everything she was teaching them, plus more. After witnessing that initial date, I was having second thoughts! But again, I had already paid her, so I went along with what she was teaching me by attending her little shop of dreams.

During this time, I received a Facebook message from a girl called Emily, she was already trained in everything but had also been working under the same franchise. It took a while for us to open up to one another as I think we weren't sure whether we could trust each other by this stage. To cut a long story short, she told me she too had been experiencing the same awful training and that she had to retrain in everything. I wasn't too sure what to believe as this other tutor was very, very convincing when it came to talking herself out of things, but she didn't know about myself and Emily chatting.

Emily invited me down to the training academy that she now had after she cut loose from this tutor and offered to help me do it alone if I needed, at the time I was so grateful but still kept getting sucked back in by this tutor. She was so good at promising the life she had. She preyed on vulnerable single mums, people that had no qualifications, no real experience in the industry and she pulled them in by offering super cheap courses!

I had everything in place for the tutor, she had sent over the work for me to send the students and a date was in place for her to come and do some training. This was the time I had worked hard and saved up the money to take myself, James, and our kids away on our first family holiday to Benidorm.

On the day I was leaving I went to work and was met by another tutor, not the one I had paid to come and teach. I assumed the tutor had filled in Julie on what she was doing. We got acquainted, I filled her in who was on the course, and off I went, leaving her with a key to my work so she could teach the students whilst I was away on holiday. I started to receive messages from the initial tutor giving me so much shit you wouldn't believe! There I was on holiday, meant to be enjoying my time off and I was receiving abusive messages like "What the fuck Vicky? You haven't even given the students the right work, none of them have done half the shit they're meant to!" I was upset and confused, she was the one that was meant to send out all the correct work for each student to complete, I wasn't trained in this at the time so how was I meant to know exactly what they were meant to have done and not done? She told me Julie was close to walking out (and looking back, I don't blame her). She had to spend one whole day doing the theory with them they should have done at home before the course and wanted extra money for it because the course was going to take her longer to teach. Apparently, it was my responsibility to pay her too! The initial tutor had told me to get eight models in for each student, which meant there were going to be 32 models. She knew exactly how many models were booked on the course as she had been receiving all the money for them directly to her bank (from me) with a follow-up message, stating who the money was from and for which student. She was so obsessed with the four lots of £745 plus the £1500 per student going into her bank (along with my fees) that she hadn't even thought through the whole process. Even worse than that she had sent someone else to teach her training course, on minimum wage. I was getting messages from the initial tutor giving me grief, messages from students, models, and Julie that it was a 'shitshow' and that I had made a huge mess of it! Julie wasn't as bad as the other tutor but was confused as hell as to how she was going to get through all this. The plan was, I booked in the allocated students, took their payments, sent it to the tutor, and told each student how many models they needed. They had to send me the course/model fees I would send to her to buy product for training and she would turn up and do the rest. It was a complete and utter mess.

BENIDORM

W hilst away on holiday, the messages from the tutor continued, constant messages of how pathetic I was, thick, stupid, and couldn't even organise something simple. It sent me into a pit of horrific anxiety attacks. I was shaking, vomiting and couldn't leave our hotel room through sheer mental exhaustion. She had the keys to my building, complaints were coming in thick and fast for refunds, and then yelled, "I'm never coming to your shitty place ever again!" and disappeared.

She wouldn't reply to my messages, calls and when I called the shop the staff was told to say she wasn't there. She left me with 20 girls booked in for the year, 160 models, and not a clue how the hell I was going to do this.

My holiday was ruined, and I was sure my business was too. I needed to get back and figure something out. I contacted Emily and explained in tears what was going on, she immediately offered to train me in the most intensive training courses over the coming weeks with all the models I needed so that I could do it myself. I beyond scared; I didn't know how the hell I was going to make this work in the first year of my business!

I had two options: try and find the money to refund everyone that the tutor was refusing to give back, or I could get my head down and do what I needed to do. I choose the latter. I took Emily up on her amazingly kind offer and she trained me to the highest standard ever. I spent weeks with her and other tutors, educating myself as much as I could. She wouldn't let me leave until I was 100% confident and had a plan. I still to this day, have no idea how I will ever repay her for her kindness. She was my guardian angel that flew in and helped me.

But even then it wasn't all rainbows and unicorns. I had to devise a plan to get my business accredited on my own. I had to get all the courses written up get them officially accredited by a training board and I was living off two hours of sleep a night trying to get everything in place to save my business. I had to work that entire year of bookings for free! The only money I was making was through treatments and any side treatments or training I had going on, just enough to pay the rent. James was working tirelessly to make sure it looked better for me and this other tutor I had working there. Well she was just making the situation ten times worse! Bringing her child into work, half-arsing her training and treatments and I was continually having to refund students on her behalf. At one point, she didn't pay her course and certificate fees to the original tutor. She made copies of the manuals and then tried to palm students off with fake certificates and accredited pictures off Google! Needless to say, she had to go, and fortunately for me, she had already hatched a plan behind my back to leave me in the shit and go solo.

So, it was just me, working for free, rearranging students to train one-on-one so I could deliver effective training that they had paid for. Luckily for me, I did get amazing reviews off the students.

Over the three years I had invested over £30,000 into my place of work to take it from a derelict property to a suitable training academy. I worked my arse off. People had nasty things to say, they would write things about me online, laugh, and say how much of a joke I was, and this wasn't even people that I had met, let alone stepped foot in my place of work. If I didn't have James at the time, I truly don't know how I would have made it through. I remember his words to me on our way home from the holiday that stuck with me forever. I was in tears and he hugged me and said, "Do you know why I'm not worried? Because you will make it work!

After everything you have been through, there's not a chance in hell you won't find a way!"

Any time now that I come up against something and question myself, I hear his words in my head. The love I have for that man, I will never be able to put into words (more on him later).

TIME MOVES ON

So, a year on, I did it! I made it through the year teaching my students for free to the best of my ability. As the feedback came in I started to grow stronger as a business, before I knew it things were doing great. I kept investing my money into my work and constantly furthering my education. I had trained an amazing woman called Angela. She came in for her training (she was one of the ones I was teaching for free) and one day she just moved in. It was like she got me; she knew what I had been through as I had been completely transparent with all the students as to why I had to move their date for training. She was brilliant and instantly fit into Empire Academy (my work) as if she had never not been there. She took on further courses with me and I trained her up to be a tutor alongside me. I found it so hard to trust again after being let down by so many people, but with Angela, she just had a way of making things go to plan. So, from then on, for the next two years, we worked alongside one another and took the business to the next level. Still to this day, she is my rock, my soul sister, my PA, my kick up the ass when I need it and above all, an amazing friend. We bossed work, we laughed, we had the best reviews from students and 2019 was my most successful year to date. I finally felt like I was doing everything I had set out to do!

Work was so successful I had people copying my business name. Let alone my posts as well. They do say imitation is the sincerest form of flattery. I did feel for them, I mean those that felt the need to copy me, they must have felt so insecure in their work, that they needed to copy someone else's hard work. No bullshitting here, for real. I felt bad they didn't have their originality. People have been copying for years, it's just a way of life, whatever sector you're in. There is a saying I love which is "They can copy the recipe, but the sauce will never taste the same."

One of the only downsides to 2019 was when my nan had to go into hospital for a hip replacement. I was worried sick about her. She was essentially my mum so the last thing I wanted was her in pain. My heart hurt for her being stuck in bed, as I knew how much she valued her independence. My Aunty Bev, my cousin Jade and myself all pulled together to provide the care she needed.

Life with James was as good as ever, we had been on multiple holidays, weekends away, concerts, you name it, we did it. My nan was always at the forefront of my mind though. Couldn't wait for her to get her new hip working so she had her independence back.

It was around this time that I completely lost contact with my mum. Throughout all the stress of myself, Jade and my Aunty Bev helping my nan, we complained that my mum and my other aunty and cousins had not been pulling their weight. My mum had Lucy yes, but she was older, much older now and she was at school most of the time. Plus my mum lived around the corner, yet we were the ones pulling our weight, we were the ones with full time jobs and families of our own. In the end there was a big row in which my other aunty told me to "Fuck off." I won't go into details as its petty and quite frankly I don't want to discuss it for my nan's sake. But this was when my mum suddenly stopped speaking to me, and as I have mentioned to this very day, she has never reached out to see any of my children, and I have been told to stay away from her and Lucy. It's quite sad really, having to answer the questions of the children on when they will see Nanny again, never getting a single text from her. As a mother myself, I genuinely cannot comprehend the though process of abandoning your own child and grandchildren, and my heart hurts sometimes that I couldn't share this next chapter with my own mother. I miss and still do, miss my baby sister Lucy so much!

NAN'S BIG NEWS

It was the 30th of November 2019, I had been to see my nan and hadn't been feeling well. I thought popping in to see her would cheer me up as it always does, but something in my mind told me I was feeling a certain way, so I nipped to the chemist and bought a pregnancy test. I brushed it off and thought *Nope, I won't be, I'll be shattered from working so much.* I got to my nans and we chatted for a while then I said I was nipping to the toilet. To our surprise we found out baby number three was on the way. I knew James would be ecstatic as he always said he wanted more kids, but I was more interested in building my empire. I was scared! However, after seeing James raise his son pretty much singlehandedly and doing an absolutely incredible job, I just knew that he would be the best dad ever.

It took about eight more tests before I believed I was actually pregnant! In fact it took many scans before I truly believed we would have a new addition. But I was, and we eventually found out we were going to be having another baby boy. On Christmas Day we announced to the other children that we had a baby on the way. To be honest, they weren't pleased. But it's certainly a funny video to look back at now. I remember my son storming out of the room at the mere thought of another sister! (I mean, how dare I run this potential risk to him).

It was 2020 and we meant business at Empire. We had so many plans, we were fully booked, and people had finally started to take my business seriously. I had put so much work into trying to get away from the tarnished name that the awful tutor left me with, that I still had a lot to prove. Even to this day of writing this book, I'm by no means where I want to be right now, but that's because I'm constantly striving for more. I remember coming out of a scan appointment and getting a call from Emily, we were (and still are) as close as ever. She called me and exclaimed, "Vicky! We have been shortlisted for 'The Training Academy of the Year' 2020!"

I was gobsmacked. I couldn't believe that little old me had been recognised for all the hard work I had put in and that we had the potential to win an award!! Ange and I were invited to attend the awards night and although we didn't win, it was the most incredible experience (even though I was about 20 weeks pregnant, fat, and shattered). The buzz was incredible, and the sense of overwhelm was real, and I knew that things were only going to get better.

THE WAVE OF COVID-19

Then the news came... there was a virus in China that was killing people. To be honest, we didn't think too much in the beginning. We thought it was probably something that would come and go, so we planned the year as normal. With students booked, we started to get messages of concern on whether we would shut. At the time, prior to me going into hospital I went in to speak to the landlord regarding the extra charges that he kept sending me and the short messages I was getting. I went in with the intention of clearing the air and hoping to find resolve. Being an arsehole, (apologies for the language, but that's putting it lightly!) he told me if I didn't like the fact he was overcharging me when I was already paying nearly a grand a month in rent and fees, without fail or the fact he was speaking down to me the way he was then I could "Get the fuck out". At this time, he had me in floods of tears, absolutely tearing me apart in front of his wife and my friend Connie. This brought on one of the worst panic attacks I had since Benidorm and ignited all the feelings of losing my business yet again. The monetary value I had put into this building, the people I had brought through his doors, the recognition I had brought to his gym from the success of my business and he treated me like a stray dog that he hated. Again, I felt so sad that it was more evident by the day, that people weren't always who they made out they were. It's a sad world when people care more for money than they do for humans and their feelings. I've always sworn that no matter how much money I ever earn in my lifetime, I would always remain humble and never treat someone that way. I would never intentionally degrade someone publicly, or in private for anything so minor that could be easily resolved amicably.

I had to find somewhere else for my academy. I had my cry and went on the hunt for a new building. Heavily pregnant, planning, and trying to figure something out, having to sign a document with him that forced me into consenting to leave all fixtures and fittings I had put into the building during my entire time there, just to get my basic things back, it got too much. My anxiety was the worst it had ever been. I pushed on, and luckily, I came across an old dental surgery, but I needed a fast turnaround. Unfortunately, it did take longer than planned but I eventually got the keys and had to start again. Yet I felt numb, I wasn't excited I was scared.

We had students eager to get in and get their courses done that they had paid for, understandably. It was roughly four weeks we had! It was so much pressure I lost all feelings towards anything and started to question my life completely. Unfortunately, the week before the announcement of the national lockdown, I had to stay off work due to the kids staying at their dad's in Bolton and him not feeling well. I had to isolate myself and the children. I received a message from a student who was having second thoughts about her course, she just decided she didn't want to do it anymore. I explained that unfortunately, we couldn't cancel her course as it was months outside the cooling off period and she had signed and agreed to official business terms that were transparent about changing your mind. I politely said that she had already completed most of the home learning and that it would be a waste for her to turn back now. She persisted about the virus and I assured her that although I was off at the moment, we would be staying open until we are told not to. Her course was months away and at this point I advised if needed, Angela could fill in, should we be allowed to work. We did end up closing the doors just before the government announcement, but only by a week maximum, if that! We did this purely for the safety of our students and clients and decided it was the right thing to do. This had absolutely no direct impact on this student at the time however, as her training was months from then. Once we realised we had to close, we contacted all students individually to let them know that unfortunately, dates would need to be deferred until further notice. All students were of course amazing about it and completely understood, all except one. The one that wanted her money back. We offered her a partial refund, minus the cost of stock and the fact she had the bulk of her coursework, offered online theory training, and the first refusal on dates once we reopened. She got aggressive, made threats, and started harassing me personally, not just on the business page but on my personal account. She messaged me repeatedly when I was in hospital with a complicated pregnancy and calling/texting up to six times in a row at any one time. Her and her husband would write comments about us on Facebook, about the business and then in April, the peak of lockdown (where travel was only allowed for absolutely essential trips) she put online a picture of her dressed for training. The academy was shut. Everywhere was shut. She continued to lie online and make slanderous comments about the staff in forums. I didn't need it right now, I was pregnant, highly vulnerable and my anxiety was sky-high. I politely asked her to get her solicitor to contact us and gave all relevant details on how to reach us, so we could liaise with them via email preferably and come to an amicable solution. I didn't hear from her again...Not then anyway.

The building I had was above a gym, I had no access to the building as the gym was shut during the lockdown. This woman had my home address (as she had visited previously) and could have sent any solicitor contact to my home address. When I was in the hospital, I was experiencing issues with the pregnancy, they were struggling to get a good reading of the baby's heartbeat and he was coming up as super small for his age. The hospital decided that I was to be induced. I put this online to let friends and family know when I would be going in. During this time, the woman had decided to start the court proceedings and have the letter sent to my work address. A place she knew I had no access to unless the landlord was there on the off chance. I did not know about this letter. She had months to do this but had waited until she knew I would be in the hospital. Something which I had no control over.

UNCONTROLLABLE FEELINGS

On 7th July 2020 I gave birth to our beautiful, tiny 5lb 13oz baby boy, Reign. He was incredible and both James and I cried as we watched him enter the world. After the birth of my son, he was whisked away to ICU due to problems he had where he stayed for two weeks. I was mortified, in complete despair. I was about to lose my business of over four years. Now I had to get a building looking professional in time for the opening date that the government had announced we could go back to work. During this time, the woman pursued her court case and preyed on someone when they were in their most vulnerable state. What kind of woman does that? As a mother herself, a grown woman, where was the empathy to wait for me to be able to defend myself in a court of law? Looking back, she did this as she knew she didn't have a leg to stand on with the business terms in place and it being over a deferred course training date, due to a global pandemic.

I arrived home without my baby and Angela had popped round to bring me some letters from work. There in black and white was a high court writ that this woman had pursued, whilst I was worried about the life of my new-born baby. She was more concerned about money. I was already in such an awful pit of depression and worry, it was so insensitive. I feel sad for her or anyone that feels the need to do such a terrible, selfish act. I often feel sad that my children may encounter people like this in life. Yes, I could have appealed it, but it was evident she needed the money more than I, I had bigger things to worry about so I look it as a learning curve and cleared the amount immediately.

Once our son was finally released from the hospital, after having to leave him there for two weeks and feeling like I had lost our baby. I slipped into a state of deep depression. How could people be so mean? What had I done to deserve all of this? All I ever wanted was to build a business that gave people a chance to start their own business and make a life of their dreams, without having to worry about where the next meal was coming from. I would allow students to pay weekly in £20s for thousand-pound courses, I would offer large discounts and free courses and do giveaways commonly for people to have the chance of a better life. Did I really deserve to be treated so poorly? Really? Even being slated on social media by a small group with a common enemy. My heart hurt and I had a harsh realisation; not everybody will treat you, the way you treat them.

I lost all motivation; I would shut myself off from the world. I rarely spoke to anyone. I just wanted to be in my bedroom with my baby. I didn't want anyone near him, I wasn't sleeping due to fear of waking and him not being there. It's crazy what lack of sleep and anxiety can do to your brain. I had started to question whether I was experiencing some postnatal depression? I started researching it and it informed me it was where you couldn't bond with your child, so I ruled that out because I was the complete opposite. If people dared suggest it, I would get defensive and say I'm tired. My brain was so exhausted that I didn't know what day it was. I disappeared completely off social media and I spent my days feeling the guilt of that on top of everything else. If it weren't for Angela holding things down for me at work, I'm not sure I would have found the motivation to ever get out of that bed. Of course James too, he was and still is so patient with me, even now when I suffer a bad day and can't seem to shake it off. He has his own life issues going on and yet he still made sure me, and the children were okay when he got home from work, but the reality was that whenever he left for work despite having my babies there with me, I felt the loneliest I had ever felt. The days rolled into one, people stopped calling, James would be working a lot to try and provide an income for us and it felt like the loneliest place in the world.

I still couldn't tell you what I needed but what I did do, was ring the doctors and got some help with some medication. Over time this started to help, and I slowly felt a little better as the days went on. It's so important that we don't hide from the face of reality and the fact that life gets hard sometimes. We all need help from time to time and in times where we cannot reach out to friends physically, I needed medication to help me get through it. There's absolutely nothing wrong with that and the stigma around it shouldn't be there. Life is hard and we could all do with a hand, even if it's for a short while.

James tried so hard to help me but if I'm being honest now, I was the only one that could help myself. But he was there, to hug me, to hold me when I needed to cry, and he never gives up on me despite how awful I was to anyone and everyone. He saw past that and saw the me from before. The semi-healed happy me I was when we first got together. He encouraged me and reminded me of why I was doing what I was doing. He was and still is, amazing.

The reason I'm explaining this, and as I said, the reason behind writing this book, was and is never for sympathy nor money. I know so many people that have gone through PND, anxiety, depression, separation anxiety, post-traumatic stress disorder, and so on and I want people to know that it's okay. I'm hoping that by explaining the things that have happened to me, and that I never really knew how to deal with, you may find a way to resolve this. I didn't know about helplines and to be honest I was probably too proud to use them then, but looking back now, I realise this could have been the best thing for me. I have since been in touch with some of them and they really do help. We don't need to suffer alone. So please use them. I'm still working out how to deal with certain aspects of life, my brain still isn't 100% but I'm quite sure after the childhood and life I have had, it never will be. I don't for one second believe that there aren't people out there that have had it a thousand times worse than me. I know there is, it is you I want to help. I want you to see that no matter the life we face, the people that try to rip away everything we have worked hard for does not define you.

You see the thing is, people who live such miserable lives, need to have someone to make them feel as low or even lower than they do. That's how they get their kicks, it makes them feel better about their lives. I used to spend hours on end in tears because someone would say something mean about me, do something nasty to me, talk shit about me or my business. I could never understand the concept of why they felt the need to hurt others and then I came to realise, most people like that are hurt themselves, they can't stand to see others doing well, being successful, being happy. It doesn't give them the right to hurt you. But I truly believe hurt people hurt people. Read that again... hurt people, hurt people. There are so many hurt people in this world, but it is not our job to fix them or fix how they treat others. It is not our job to fall victim to what they decide to put us through.

I write this chapter with my beautiful six-month-old baby on my knee, finally feeling grateful for everything that I have overcome.

I have my academy that I'm still working on, and I have met some of the most amazing people along my journey. I have the goals I still want to achieve, but I'm grateful for the ones that I have already reached. I sit in my beautiful home that just five years ago I could have only imagined living in. My relationship with my first two children's dad, is now great. We have learned over the years how to co-parent and although we still have our differences, I will always respect him for being a present father to our children. I have an amazing partner that after four years hasn't given up on me, a couple of loyal friends, and a hell of a lot of gratitude for still being here to tell this story. I may have lost my own family, but with the help of James, we created our own and his wider family welcomed me into theirs. A real family that stands strong for one another, a family that helps in times of need, a family that will help you out with the children when you need a break. This was so alien to me. It's something I had never had, and I will be forever grateful for being blessed now with what I have.

What happened in my life hasn't happened to me, but for me. Every single issue I have faced has made me stronger in some way. It has had to happen in order for me to become the person I need to be. The people I have met have shown me what I never want to be like. The issues I have faced are what I want to raise awareness about. The relationships I have had proved to me that although it is hard, it's never the end. There are still good people out there that will love you, scars, flaws, and all. We have (and are still, at the time of writing this book) dealing with a global pandemic. There are no rules on how we deal with that, let alone when we find other obstacles thrown at us as well. Some of us don't know if our businesses l make it through the (hopefully) final lockdown with a business on the other side of it. So many businesses can't and won't be able to survive, some can't afford to reopen and this year has been the toughest and most historical year that I, or anyone in my generation, have lived. However, I know one thing for sure and that is I won't ever give up again! I still have a huge amount to prove to my children and now, with another set of beautiful little eyes looking up to me, calling me Mummy, I have no choice but to make it.

Mental health is constantly on the rise, the statistics are at the highest they have been in a long time right now. As humans, we are not biologically designed to live with no human contact. We are not designed to live in fear, we are not designed to live in fight or flight mode constantly. When I walk down the street, I want to smile at someone and hopefully, they'll smile back. I want to say "Hello" to that little old lady who may not have spoken to someone in months. Now we can't and it's difficult, but it won't last forever, no bad times do.

If you want a life you've never had, you must do something you have never done. I am so passionate about pushing people outside of their comfort zones. Yes, it's easy to stay in that 9–5 job that you hate, because it pays the bills. But are you happy? Are you happy when your co-worker is moaning in your ear, about how cold it is, sitting in a miserable office or workplace that you hate or when the 'every month new diet starter' is throwing her lettuce at your head because she's in a mood that she's on a diet *again* this month? You can stay there and never take a risk. It's the easy way and lots of people do it. They do it because it's just that *easy*. But what if, just what if you do decide to be brave and step outside that zone, just one step, one risk and you decide to go for it? You have an unlimited number of opportunities awaiting you, you can do or be anything you want. All you must do is be brave, bold and find something you're passionate about. Ignore the negativity, ignore the naysayers, the people that can't dream as big as you and go for it!

What's the worst that can happen? You fail? I don't see it as a failure, I see it as a lesson. We fall, we get back up. No matter how many times it takes. I can bet once you have had a taste of that freedom and that independence, that fire in your belly, you'll never want to go back to conforming like everybody else. I dare you to take a risk outside that comfort zone today. When people ask me how I do anything new I come up with, I simply tell them "I took a risk" and this is what I want each and every one of you to do. There's room at the top for everyone. Take that risk.

Today I look at it all as a blessing.

Thank you for showing me pain, it taught me strength.

Thank you for showing me tears, it taught me to smile.

Thank you for showing me loss, it taught me appreciation.

Thank you for showing me lessons, it taught me direction.

I like this quote from James M Meston, "Success has a price tag on it and the price tag reads: courage, determination, discipline risk taking, perseverance, and consistency – doing the right things for the right reasons and not just when we feel like it."

I'm just a girl from a little town called Blackpool, I decided to make a promise to myself, my children and family, that we will never go without again. The only thing I did differently to anyone else is I took a risk outside that warm comfort zone, said yes to any opportunity that came up and I took the losses as lessons. But I never gave up, despite how hard it got.

Sometimes when you're a mum every day, doing everything all alone, as I was previously, it can be hard to take in the special moments of our children's life. We sit on our phones and look at other people with better lives, working, or even catching up with friends in a bid to stay sane. We snap at the children because we feel so tired and have been so drained with life or from working so much. You feel like they don't understand. To clean, cook, work, raise two (now four since being with James) children singlehandedly. Dress them smartly, keep in touch with friends, do the laundry, do their homework, and reading (and currently home schooling too!) You push yourself to physical and mental growth in a bid to progress through life. Know that the mum guilt you feel sometimes, is not irregular and we all go through this. I'm so grateful that I have James in my life now to help me, because I do truly understand what it is like to do things alone, but I still get mum guilt too! We are doing the best we can and that's what matters the most.

I own a business that runs training courses, I work hard, I commit, and I don't give up, no matter how many times I fall. Nobody ever said it was going to be easy and, in my eyes, I'm still so far from where I want to be, but I'm here, I'm alive and I'm grateful. When you suffer with a mental illness or a mental health problem, people that tell you that you 'don't look poorly' or 'you can't suffer with anxiety, because you're so chatty'. Just because you don't see someone's pain, please don't let it make you assume that they do not have pain inside that they are dealing with every single day. As humans we need to understand the true meaning of being kind and understand that so many people are fighting battles that none of us know about.

I made a promise a while ago that no matter what anybody throws at me, I will deal with it. I will rise. I may cry, I still have days that I suffer from my anxiety, but I have three sets of little eyes looking up to me, they call me Mummy (and a stepson) and I'll be damned if I'm going to let anything or anyone, get in the way of achieving the best I can for those special people, that saved me when I needed saving the most.

Know that you are loved, you are special, you have a unique talent of being YOU. Nobody else is the same as you, nobody else's story is exactly like yours and if you let it be, that's pretty fucking special right?

You can do this! I love you with all my heart.

Vicky x

FINAL NOTE FROM THE AUTHOR

I guess you're wondering how I got out of those dark places? For a long time, I didn't know. It was just auto pilot until it got too much. I eventually did it by keeping so busy, that my head and brain didn't have time to process any other thoughts or feelings that I was going through. I would work ridiculous hours just so that I was never alone with my thoughts. I would keep myself occupied by going for walks with music on to drown out the thoughts or doing jobs for other people. I know that sounds a little bit selfish, but by helping other people, it made me feel a little less vulnerable and a little more in control of my life and my situation. I mean if I can make somebody else feel better then why wouldn't I? I would often help others that were in the same or a similar situation, in a bid to try and make my own life feel less miserable. Again, writing that makes me feel a little selfish, but I thought I was doing something good. I searched for healing in many different places through drugs and drink in my younger years; spiritual guidance, meditation, crystal healing and even so much as praying to a God, that I'm even not sure I believed in.

Even now, sometimes I will go and drive in the car alone with my thoughts and just try to deal with them, so that I don't project them on to anybody else. So many that know me, wouldn't believe the majority of this story existed and wouldn't believe how much I suffer daily with anxiety attacks, separation anxiety and the feelings of neglect and worry of being left behind. They see a bright, successful businesswoman who is intellectually knowledgeable, chatty and friendly and knows how to run a business. The work face I call it, but what you see on the outside isn't always what you will see on the inside and I think it's really important that people know that. Eventually, I found my coping mechanisms through having a positive mindset and keeping myself busy, but also by facing my fears head on and learning how to cope with them through my own special means, such as meditation and surrounding myself with the best kinds of people that lift me up.

As I mentioned earlier, I still couldn't tell you how I managed to get over everything that happened to me. I'm not sure if I ever have or will, but I do know that every single day is a learning curve and all you can do is continue to try. There are always going to be triggers or obstacles that you will face in times of scarcity or in situations you are put in that will be uncontrollable. Some of the people I love the most pay the price for those fears to this day, even though they have nothing at all to do with them being there in the first place. But the best that we can do is take one day at a time, keep pushing forward and remember that we aren't alone, and we aren't victims of situations that we have been through. They haven't defined us they have moulded us. They have created us into the people that I believe are truly some of the kindest, big-hearted, and beautiful souls that I tend to come across. It's always the ones that have been through the most that tend to be the ones that will do the most for others. I have been without, I have witnessed things I will never be able to unsee, I have had bad things happen to me that I will never be able to take away. But I do know one thing; if I ever found a person in that situation myself, I would do everything in my power to ensure their safety and ensure they never went without. Because I know exactly how it feels to be where they are. I think that's the difference between people that have been through things and people that haven't. They will never understand the depths of despair that you feel when you are at your lowest point in life. I decided to write this book as a means of therapy. As I close the chapter on this book, I intend to leave every story inside this book and never let it affect me again. You can do this too with me if you like? Or write it down on some paper, everything! And then burn it and watch that new beginning start again. I am physically closing the chapter of my life that I no longer want to be a part of. Whether or not I'll be able to do that is another story, but all I can do, is keep pushing, until I make it out the other side.

Now my new journey begins...

SPECIAL THANKS

I would like to take time out, to thank some extra people in my life that I have been blessed with and that have helped me bring this book to life.

Firstly, I would like to thank my gorgeous (and he knows it!) partner James for his constant support. For pushing me to believe in myself, for always having my back (even on the days I'm at my worst and can't get out of bed). For telling me how beautiful I am, even when I'm ugly crying. For his patience with me, whenever I get some crazy idea in my head and my head doesn't leave my phone or laptop. Most of all I want to thank him for blessing us with our beautiful baby boy and for being the best daddy and role model, he could possibly be.

Secondly, I want to deeply apologise to my children, my beautiful Rico, Reign and Laicey for always being so busy, for missing out on movie nights and baking days, even parents evenings through working so much. For not being as attentive as I should be and for always being tired and stressed. They have held me together over the years (and driven me crazy!) and I haven't always been the best mum, but I promise that everything I do, I do for you all. Without these special people, I would truly be lost, you are my reason why, you are my life and I love you all, with every inch of my being. Thank you for giving me a reason to wake up every single day.

Thank you to my beautiful nan, for showing me strength, courage, and for never judging me by my mistakes. For always being the only constant in my life, for sharing every single special moment with me whilst being my number one fan and finally, for always believing in everything I do (she didn't know about this book until she got a copy. I have kept it secret!)

Thank you, to Leanne from Red Pencil Ltd for her incredible work ethic in editing and for working alongside me to bring my book to life. With a thirteen-hour time difference she has still managed to turn things around faster than expected and put up with my million questions. She has worked with me patiently whilst understanding that this book was not an easy one to write, that I made lots of (assumingly annoying!) changes constantly and her kindness and patience with me, I am truly grateful for.

Sehar Tahir, you are incredible, you are truly so kind, your patience with me throughout this book with regards to changes and waiting for everything else to be complete before you start and finish you design has been impeccable. Your artwork stole my heart the moment I saw it and I am truly grateful for you. Again, you have also helped me bring my book to life, without you it would not have been possible. My book cover is the face of my story and you brought that to life. Thank you.

Finally, I would like to thank you, the readers of my book, without you I wouldn't have the strength to have told this story. I truly hope just one person can take something from this story. I hope I give you an ounce of motivation or strength to see there is always light at the end of the tunnel. Stay with it.

Please, if you have enjoyed reading my book, I would greatly appreciate it if you could take the time out to leave a review on Amazon for me or on my Facebook page Dreaming of an Empire. On the Facebook page you will get to learn so much more about the behind-the-scenes stuff and pictures of those I love the most. I truly hope it has helped just one person at least. Thank you.

Before I leave you, please take the time to read the following poem that my amazingly talented nan wrote for me a while ago. It is something so dear to me:

My darling Vicky, you mean so much to me.

The reason is when you were born–you stole my heart you see.

I watched you grow as the years rolled by, then college beckoned you.

But for that you needed money, so what were you to do?

You simply got yourself a job–cleaning bedrooms and toilets too.

You worked so hard at college, then fast for university too.

My Viktoria, in cap and gown–I was so proud of you!

Day and night, you worked so hard burning the midnight oil, but looking back was it worth it? All that sweat and toil.

I guess it was, for look at you, a businesswoman of high regard, a property owner too.

You did it, Vicky, I knew you would.

Your dream has now come true.

You've made me so very proud, just like you promised to.

So, follow your dream as far as you can, be happy and healthy too. I will always be with you, all the way–watching and loving you.

(Copyright to Margret Jean Medlock)

Printed in Great Britain
by Amazon

58781734R00073